THE SHORT AND BLOODY HISTORY OF KNIGHTS

CONTENTS

WHAT IS A KNIGHT?

Everyone thinks they know about knights: rich guys in flashy armor tearing around the countryside, killing excess dragons, rescuing damsels trapped in towers, and knocking each other off of horses with long poles at special tournaments!

So why write yet another book? Simple! I wanted to find out all the stuff we don't know. Like, where did knights buy their armor? How much did it cost? How easy was it to move, let alone fight, covered from head to foot in metal? What did they get paid fighting for the king? What did they eat? Where —and with whom—did they live? Were they really the brave, noble guys we are led to believe, or were some wimpy, cowardly, and dishonest? I'm going to try to tell you what knights were really like—warts and all—and what it was like to be one.

Career Knights

The first thing to remember is that knights were the very first mercenaries (paid soldiers). They were paid, usually with large plots of land, to fight for their lord or king.

The second thing to remember is that they were supposed to conduct themselves according to a strict code of behavior. This was called chivalry.

Last and most important, the knights were part of a way of life, called the feudal system, that existed in Europe. Basically the feudal system helped a king obtain thousands of men for the wars he always fought. His barons and earls, in exchange for vast areas of land, pledged to provide armies on request. These barons and earls gave smaller parcels of their land to knights who, in return, promised to supply men (peasants) to do the fighting. In return for doing this, the knight assigned these peasants much smaller pieces of land to provide food for their families—and the knight's family.

How to Be a Knight

But who got to be a knight? For starters, before you get too excited, you had to be the son of a knight. Around the age of twelve, you went to another knight's house to learn how to knight—so to speak. The knight in question started you off as a page (young attendant) and then as a personal servant, called a squire. This duty involved grooming his horses, polishing his armor, and even serving him his breakfast, lunch, and dinner. In return he taught you how to ride horses and fight at the same time, as well as the code of chivalry as mentioned above.

Knight Time

Eventually, when the knight in charge of you decided you were ready, it was time for the big day. First you took a special bath in holy water and said prayers and stuff. Then you had to

put on an outfit of white clothes and pray all night in front of your nice new armor as it sat on the altar. Just like Christmas, you weren't allowed to touch it until morning. After all of your relatives and friends had arrived at the church, you put on your armor while the priest blessed it and you. That done, another knight gave you a whack on the shoulder with the flat (hopefully) part of his sword and presto, you became a full-fledged knight.

EARLY KNIGHTS

The British usually like to think that they invented knights. They boast Sir Galahad, Sir Lancelot, and those other guys who hung around the Round Table. But, much to my dismay, I must break the news that it looks like knights were a German idea. Even the very word knight comes from the German *knecht*. Bad news!

In the Middle Ages (roughly A.D. 500 to A.D. 1500), a bunch of German-speaking peoples called the Franks occupied the land that later became France. In the fifth century, when the Roman Empire began to decline and fall, these Franks, under Clovis I, took advantage. By A.D. 494, all of northern France had fallen under their control. Then Clovis got religion and decided to become a Catholic. He insisted that all the Franks became Catholic, too, a move that united the various Frankish tribes into one people.

So what's all this got to do with knights? Please be patient.

In the meantime, the religion of Islam had been founded on the Arabian Peninsula. Its followers, called Muslims, had been slowly building a large empire in the Middle East and North Africa. By the eighth century, the massive Muslim army was ready to hit Spain. The Islamic soldiers found themselves sunning on the beaches of southern France by the following year. Something had to be done to prevent the Muslims from taking over all of western Europe. This task fell to the Franks, who had the most powerful medieval kingdom.

Charles Martel in France, King Alfred in England, and a German called Henry the Fowler (King Henry I) provided loads of horses to help repel the raiders. Their cavalry (soldiers on horseback) became the first to use stirrups. These new devices enabled them to gallop much faster than before (without crippling themselves in very embarrassing places). So as they swept into mainland France in 716, the Muslims were stopped in their tracks by the cavalry of Charles Martel, the Franks' leader.

Warhorses, however, were expensive and learning how to use them well took years of training. To support his cavalry, the now ever-so-popular Martel gave his best soldiers lumps of land (that he had snatched from the Catholic Church). They didn't even have to tend the land, as they had dependent peasants to farm the plots for them. This was just the very beginning of feudalism. The only condition to receive land was that these soldiers had to agree to fight for Martel, no questions asked, equipped with their own horses and any weapons they might need.

During the latter half of the eighth century, the mighty and very famous Charlemagne doubled the Frankish kingdom, continually pushing back the mega-miffed Muslims wherever he and his soldiers came across them.

But what has this got to do with knights?

Well, Charlemagne's world-famous cavalry, taken from the most noble of Frankish families, were the first real knights, thus making knighthood a military rank. Being rich, these guys had no problem supplying their own horses, chain mail, helmets, swords, clothes, and other stuff required to fight wars—right down to enough bag lunches to last up to three months at a time. These guys made the most savage, cruel, efficient, and formidable army that you could ever have had the misfortune to bump into.

Knight's Service

From this Frankish kingdom, the feudal system developed and spread throughout the western world. As I explained briefly before, it worked like this: every scrap of land in those days belonged to the sovereign prince—be he king, duke, marquis, or count. This prince issued fiefs (land given in return for military service) to his barons. The barons gave pieces of their fiefs to knights (or vassals) who pledged to fight for them and, therefore, the sovereign prince. This land supported fifteen to thirty peasant families who were not allowed to work (or do much else) anywhere else! The soldiers, most male members of these families, had to fight whomever, wherever, and whenever their master needed them and guard the big boss's castle from attack. All in all the peasants spent at least forty days a year in his lordship's service—for no pay.

This system actually meant that throughout Europe, at the drop of his crown, the king or lord could assemble a huge army (of admittedly not-always-very-good soldiers) to fight whomever he pleased.

Brotherhood

So, due to this feudalism business, which spread quickly through Europe, these knights felt a sort of brotherhood with their foreign counterparts. By the eleventh century, knighthood in Europe had become hereditary (passed down from father to son), as long as the new boy accepted the same responsibilities as his dad to their overlord.

Dub Dub

Knights from the eleventh century onward had to be dubbed (named) at special ceremonies (swords on shoulders, etc.). There they swore an oath to defend the Catholic Church and to protect the womenfolk, widows, orphans, pets, sick, and old. The swearing part was easy, as it turned out. Some knights misused their authority to rob the poor, to take advantage of the women, and to live in luxury at the expense of everyone else.

Knights' Rules

The whole idea of how a knight should behave went under the general term of "chivalry." (Chivalry comes from *chevalerie,* the old French word for soldiers on horses.) Every knight was supposed to be bound by the rules of chivalry, which were as follows:

1. A knight never tells lies.
2. He defends the Catholic Church (headed by the pope).
3. He defends the weak, suppresses the wicked, and honors God with noble acts (juggling? acrobatics?).
4. He is brave and loyal in defense of the knight who knighted him and that knight's lady.
5. Women (read "wealthy women") are held in high regard (even though they had no legal rights or power).
6. A knight never has an affair with another knight's girl.
7. The object in battle is always to capture the enemy, not to kill him.
8. Knights never fight during the pre–Easter period of Lent and even get a couple of days off at Christmas.
9. If a nobleman is captured, he has to be treated according to his rank.

For Instance

In 1356 the Black Prince (Prince Edward of England) captured the king of France, John II, at Poitiers. The prince actually served the king at his own table and kept him in the most luxurious prison that London, the capital of England, could offer.

How to Build a Feudal Army

First of all, knowing that he had to get an army together for a specific battle, a king first decided how many soldiers he needed (give or take a hundred). On the principle that you don't need a sledgehammer to crack a walnut, there was no point calling up 5,000 men to stop a brawl. After sizing up the battle, the king put the word out to all his earls and lords. They, in turn, supplied men in proportion to their quota (which depended on how much land they'd received in the first place). Clear so far?

The earl then called on the knights to whom he had given land (fiefs) and told them how many men he needed. If there were enough soldiers available, many of these knights opted to pay scutage (tax that allowed them to buy their way out of fighting). With this kind of income, the king could buy the better services of professional soldiers! This was the beginning of armies as we know them today. (Earls, by the way, couldn't buy their way out of their own duty to fight—unless deemed too old, too young, too feeble, or too crazy.) If the battle or siege went on for more than the free initial forty days, the king paid the knights and soldiers wages. Earls, naturally, were expected to do it for nothing.

The armies often found themselves in interesting situations. In the wars of 1294 between the English king Edward I and the Welsh rebels, the earl of Lancaster, who lorded over 263 knightly fiefs, turned up to fight for the king with only fifty men. The earl of Norfolk, who also had 263 fiefs, pitched in with only twenty-eight men, and the greatest baron of Devon, Hugh Courtney, with 92 fiefs, only managed twelve men—

and so on. This wasn't a problem. The king received a lot of scutage money from those who preferred to pay up rather than go to war. The king could then distribute all the extra cash to the knights who'd showed up with their fair share of soldiers.

In the case of these Welsh wars, the campaign continued well over the forty days, meaning that the king ran out of the old scutage money fairly quickly. This is where being able to jack up the taxation of the whole population becomes so convenient. Anyway, it all worked out just fine in the end (if you weren't Welsh). Edward kept his troops clothed and fed while the rebels eventually ended up starving in the hills.

Big Rewards

Most wars were profitable for knights and barons. Many captured their French counterparts and sold the prisoners back to their own side for some quick cash (enough to build an entire castle). Every large house boasted French silverware, furs, linens, and closets full of beautiful clothes —bought with the ransom or stolen from a foreign home during a war.

By the Way

A small band of civilians, called camp followers, followed armies to the battlefields in order to sell them food and wine. After the battle, they went over the stiffs, especially those of the dead knights, and swiped jewelry and valuables. Rotten job, but somebody had to do it.

KNIGHTS AND RELIGION

Religion in the Middle Ages had its hands in just about everything—right up to its elbows.

It's important to realize that those who went into the higher ranks of the Catholic Church came from the same stratum of society as the knights—usually the better-off landowners. The church, by the way, provided an acceptable alternative for the landed gentry's sons and daughters (especially the ones they couldn't marry off). Very often a knight called on his brother in the church to help him out and vice versa. If you go into any really old church in England, you can still see from the stained-glass windows and these lying-down statues of knights and their wives just how important they were in those days.

God Rules

God was everywhere in medieval Europe. Although only a fraction of the buildings we see these days existed then, there were even more churches, chapels, and monasteries. The very rich knights often supported the church—paying for a new spire here or a new roof there—in return for showy family tombs or their pictures on the church walls.

But despite living together fairly well, the church began to get more and more fed up with the endless arguments that often led to wars between rival knights. They'd had enough of armed "robber barons" raiding their villages, burning the monasteries, running off with their livestock, and killing anyone who had a problem with it. The church was also angry with those overlords that hid in massive fortified castles and bled the surrounding countryside dry.

At one stage the Catholic Church tried to make the

warring knights agree to a Truce of God. Church officials threatened to excommunicate (evict from the church) anyone who wouldn't participate. Then, in 1041, at the Council of Nice, they went even further by forbidding war on Sundays. Fine from Monday through Saturday, but not on Sunday. The church later extended the period to last from Thursday to Sunday, which is crazy when you think about it. The knights, bless 'em, saw this as interference in their business. Most of them wanted nothing to do with the truce.

In 1077 Pope Gregory VII put his big ecclesiastical foot in it, ordering that everyone from peasant to king had to do as he said. The knights particularly, he declared, must obey whatever

WAIT A MINUTE— IT'S ONLY SUNDAY

the church told them—or else! Then Gregory, apparently a really tough guy, decided it was time to lead a Christian army against the non-Christians of the world, particularly the Muslims. He vowed to relieve Jerusalem, a city that had been taken over by the Muslims. Pope Gregory had heard that Christian pilgrims, on their way to the Holy Land (ancient

Israel and ancient Palestine) to worship, were being captured and sold as slaves, which was darned rude even then.

Pilgrims

Although most people in the Middle Ages hardly knew what went on outside their villages (let alone in the rest of the world), a constant stream of European pilgrims traveled to and from the Holy Land, particularly Jerusalem. Once there, they fell down in front of holy relics (the remains of significant religious objects), such as the tongue of Saint Mark, Jesus' crown of thorns, and hair from the head of John the Baptist.

Unfortunately Pope Gregory VII died in 1085, so it was up to his replacement, Pope Urban II, to continue Gregory's fight. The Byzantine* emperor, Alexius I Comnenus, who'd lost many provinces to the Muslims, wrote a remarkable letter to Pope Urban and a bunch of lords. He asked them to get armies together to help him. In the letter, he described some of the ghastly atrocities committed by some Muslims. (Some of the things they did to the grown-up Christians were too awful for even me to describe.) Just to sweeten the pill, however, Alexius also happened to mention that if saving Christians from their terrible fate and rescuing Jerusalem didn't coax the crusaders, other rewards awaited them. The Holy Land, he claimed, abounded with fabulous treasures, theirs for the taking. Thus, the Crusades began. The knights saw immediately that they could not only satisfy the continually whiny church but also make loads of money.

* *The Byzantine Empire was formed from the eastern part of the Roman Empire.*

ANYONE FOR A CRUSADE?

Not only soldiers but religions clashed in the Crusades. Muslims wanted to make everyone else think like they did. The crusaders, who were Christians, didn't like this at all and wanted everyone to think like them. So in 1095 Pope Urban realized that it was time to stop whining about these differences and do something about them. This is how the whole idea of the Crusades came about.

By the Way

You'll see the term *infidel,* meaning one who has no faith, used to describe the Muslims. The joke is that the Christians stole the term from the Muslims who first used it to describe the Christians.

In addition, the Muslims fighting the crusaders were of Turkish origin and had taken over lands in what is now Turkey, eastern Europe, and the Middle East.

The First Crusade

You could say that the First Crusade kicked off at about 3:35 P.M. on Tuesday, November 27, 1095, in a great big field just outside the walls of the French city of Clermont-Ferrand. (The cathedral wasn't big enough to hold everyone.) The furious pope yelled at the massed crowds that enough was enough. The Muslims continually had invaded Christian lands, ruining the churches and torturing the pilgrims. They had reached Jerusalem, the most precious jewel in the Christian crown. It was time, the pope cried, for the sword to be in partnership with religion.

The response was so enthusiastic that, at the end of the meeting, the 300 assembled bishops rushed home to recruit crusaders. The church made some knights into priests. It told them that they were on active service for the defense of the faith. The knights actually began to believe that, by going to rescue Jerusalem, they were working for God. The groups of crusaders had to make their own way, at their own expense, to the Byzantine city of Constantinople (now Istanbul, Turkey). There, they planned to meet up and set out together to attack the Muslims and anyone else who needed a lesson. After they succeeded, they planned to snatch back the city of Jerusalem.

God and Money

We know from Pope Urban's famous letter that the Crusades offered more to knights than teaching the Muslims a lesson, or doing God a favor, or earning themselves eternal salvation and a nice little corner in heaven. Sure, these things and the fame that they would bring were pretty attractive, but on their own they weren't appealing enough. It took more to make people want to risk dying in unimaginable ways in faraway lands. Anyway, who would look after things back home—the farmlands, the peasants, and, much more to the point, the wife?

No, there had to be more to it than that.

Land Ahoy

You see, apart from the treasure, the crusaders also claimed huge tracts of land and made fortunes by opening up trade routes from the cities that were about to be freed of Muslim control.

By the Way

Author Geoffroi de Villehardouin described the fantastic wealth of some knights after the Crusades. For a laugh, one knight plowed the land surrounding his castle and filled the ditches with silver coins to make his lands glitter. Another knight had thirty horses burned alive for a bet (why not race them, like everyone else?). Another wealthy crusader cooked a massive banquet over millions of candles just to prove that it was possible.

Crusading for All

In 1096 five huge armies of knights and noblemen set off, mostly from the land of modern-day France and Germany. Alongside the noblemen traveled well over 20,000 ordinary people. They were led by a middle-aged weirdo—a French priest named Peter the Hermit. They all gave up everything (which on the whole was not that much) to join the holy campaign and to walk more than 2,000 miles to Jerusalem. This Crusade was later referred to as the Peasants' Crusade.

By the Way

Peter the Hermit, although he looked filthy, was regarded as almost divine. The adoring throngs even stole hairs from Peter's donkey (soon bald) and kept them as religious relics, because he looked and smelled like his master.

Roast Turkey

As the peasant crusaders passed through Germany and on through Hungary and the Balkans, thousands more joined. These like-minded peasants had been whipped into religious fervor by their leaders. All in all, the peasant army traveling east numbered as many as 50,000. But religious Crusades are funny things. These so-called committed Christians thought nothing of robbing and looting Turkish Christians whom they passed on the way. There were even reports that the French contingent barbecued little baby Turks on spits when they got hungry (the French always did have weird taste in food). The mob had turned unruly and were perpetually hungry. They pillaged practically any town they came across—friendly or otherwise. It became clear that most of the peasant crusaders had gone on the journey because it seemed like a better option than staying behind and starving.

Bed and Who's Breakfast?

Remember, the crusaders had to travel through other famine-struck regions to reach their destination. While trudging across some remote parts of France and Germany, it was not unusual for the peasant crusaders to stay at an inn only to have their throats cut and then be eaten by the locals.

Turkish Delight

A bunch of Flemish peasant soldiers called Tafurs traveled with Peter the Hermit. They wound up, in 1097, joining the main crusader army in their attack on the almost unattackable city of Antioch (Syria). Owing to the size of the army (100,000 plus), most of the soldiers were starving in the area's arid, unyielding landscape, except the Tafurs. The Tafurs simply collected, cooked, and ate the carcasses of the dead Turks. When they ran out of dead ones, they hunted live ones purely for food.

Anyone for Blood?

But the going got tough for crusaders everywhere. At one point, 6,000 German and Italian crusaders captured a castle called Xerigordon. The Muslim leader, or sultan, promptly surrounded it and cut off its only water supply. After a few days in the blazing heat, the crazed crusaders became so thirsty that they emptied the blood out of their own horses and drank it. After eight days, they gave in, and the Muslims slaughtered anyone who wouldn't renounce Christianity.

Later, at another deserted fortress at Civeton, near Constantinople, the occupying crusaders, who formed a large part of Peter the Hermit's enormous peasant army, marched out to meet the Turks, who were preparing to attack. Unfortunately, they walked straight into an ambush. With the Turks hot on their heels, the crusaders scurried back to the fortress. A few thousand escaped, but the rest of the fleeing soldiers, as well as the women and children within the walls, were hacked to death. All that was left was a mountain of bones. Later, when rebuilding the fortress walls, the Turks used those bones like pebbles to fill the cracks in the huge stones (waste not, want not). The walls still stand today as a tomb to the dead crusaders.

NOW WHAT CAN WE FILL THOSE CRACKS WITH?

Peter the Hermit was not among those killed. He had been away negotiating with the Byzantine emperor Alexius. Most of his army was destroyed. The whole Peasants' Crusade turned sour as very few of these ill-equipped commoners ever reached the Middle East. The ones who did reach their destination fought so poorly that the Turks made mincemeat of them. Practically none of the peasants saw the eventual Christian takeover of Jerusalem in 1099.

The nobleman army, made up of real knights on the other hand, had it a little easier. They swept through Constantinople like a hot knife through butter. In 1097 they approached their first major target of Nicaea, the Turkish capital (now called Isnik, located on the Asian mainland of Turkey).

Siege of Nicaea

At some time or another, every crusader had to cross the Bosporus strait (a waterway that separates the European part of Turkey from the Asian part of Turkey). The waterway also divides the narrow land between the Mediterranean and Black Seas.

In order to move on easily, they felt they had to capture the mighty city of Nicaea. Heavily fortified and protected by a hundred towers, the city was, therefore, almost impregnable. The crusaders besieged the city for two weeks, but the Turks inside wouldn't surrender that easily. Their boss, the sultan, was away with most of his army fighting some rival Muslims at the time (they were all at it in those days). He came back as soon as he heard, to try to besiege the besiegers.

The Nicaean Turks' favorite trick, when bored with firing their bows and arrows, was to lower iron hooks over the massive walls and try to hoist up the bodies of the dead or wounded crusaders that lay at the bottom—like fishing for plastic ducks at the fair. If the Turks succeeded, they'd reel the bodies up to the top, strip them of their armor, and fling the naked carcasses back at their enemies below. The crusaders, not to be outdone, chopped off the heads of the

Turkish corpses and prisoners and catapulted them back over the walls. Take that!

The occupants of Nicaea refused to submit as they were still getting supplies by boat across Lake Ascania. But the Byzantine navy eventually turned up and put a stop to that. The head Turk, realizing the game was almost up, made an agreement with the Byzantine admiral that they could have the city as long as they didn't harm anyone. This really annoyed the rest of the crusaders, who'd been looking forward to a good slaughter.

After many similar battles and sieges, the crusaders eventually reached Jerusalem (in 1099), which was under Egyptian control. After a short but bloody siege, they lost patience and jumped over the walls, massacring almost everyone inside. Then the crusaders went home, leaving a Frankish duke called Godfrey de Bouillon in charge.

The Second Crusade

Once in charge, Godfrey promptly established four Christian states or counties—Jerusalem, Edessa, Antioch, and Tripoli. The most powerful, Jerusalem, was in a real mess after all that fighting. But the Muslims were furious and certainly weren't going to lie down and take this invasion lightly.

Gradually regrouping, they formed a massive army under a new leader, Nur ad-Din. They hit back by taking Edessa in 1144. The pope of the day wouldn't stand for this upset. He begged the new generation of knights to get out their swords and give it another try—the Second Crusade. This time the rallying call and the success of the last campaign attracted even more recruits. The Holy Roman Emperor, Conrad III, led a German army from Nuremberg in 1147. The French force left shortly after, and both armies were severely ambushed on the way. Although a few reached Jerusalem, most of the second crusaders simply went home.

This cheered up the Muslims immensely and left them free to regroup. By 1169, under the mighty Saladin, they were ready to get back the lands they had lost. Surrounding Jerusalem on three sides, Saladin's massive army overran the whole kingdom. All the knights who had remained in Jerusalem were beheaded to teach them a lesson (which it probably did!).

The Third Crusade

Back home in Europe everyone was furious. Very soon, in 1191, the Third Crusade started on its way to get Saladin. This time the Holy Roman Emperor, Frederick I, French king Philip II, and England's Richard I gathered the largest crusader army ever seen. Unfortunately Frederick died on the way and most of his army meandered home to Germany. The other two kings failed to capture Jerusalem—or anything else.

The Fourth and Fifth Crusades

The next two Crusades were rather pathetic attempts. The fourth, in 1202, only managed to capture and plunder Constantinople. The fifth achieved absolutely nothing and ended with the crusader army putting up its hands and running home.

Kid Knights

This is where the whole thing gets really weird. In 1212 thousands of French and German kids, disgusted at the knights' lack of success in getting back the Holy Land, decided to give it a shot. In doing so themselves, they hoped to become true Knights of the Cross.

In France the Children's Crusade was led by a fast-talking twelve-year-old shepherd boy called Stephen. He promised his "men" that, when they got to the Mediterranean coast, the sea would dry up before them, like it had for Moses, and a sign would appear saying "Jerusalem this Way" (honest!). They were glad they wouldn't need boats to make the first part of the journey to the Holy Land.

Thirty thousand children, most under the age of twelve, set off from Vendôme, France, behind this medieval Pied Piper. By the time they got to the sea at Marseilles, many of the youngsters had dropped out due to the severe July heat.

Anyway, they waited and waited but, guess what, the Mediterranean Sea stayed as wet and as deep as ever. Eventually a couple of rich merchants took pity on the children and hired seven ships to take them to the Holy Land. The poor little misguided kids were never heard of again. Well, not for twenty years, when the true story emerged. Two of the ships went down in a storm. The rest of the children were surrounded almost as soon as they stepped off the boats and promptly sold as slaves to Muslim traders.

The Last Crusades

Frederick II, the new Holy Roman Emperor, thought he'd try a crusade in 1215 but didn't actually manage to get it together until 1227. The poor old guy hadn't traveled very far out of port before he fell sick and had to go back home, leaving his army. The pope, who'd been waiting impatiently for the

Crusade to kick off, lost his cool. Showing a severe lack of sympathy, he excommunicated the sick emperor (which meant he couldn't be a Christian any more). This didn't stop our Freddie, however, for in 1228, when feeling better, he set off again to find his army. When he got to where he thought they'd be—they weren't there. Apparently most of them got fed up waiting and left. Freddie therefore made a deal with the Egyptian Sultan al-Kamil and succeeded in getting the kingdom of Jerusalem back for the crusaders. Despite this, he was still shunned by the pope, believe it or not, who even sent a little Crusade to try to steal Frederick's Italian possessions while he was away.

After a couple more small Crusades, the last one departed in 1270, when Louis IX set off with his knights to capture the city of Tunis. This ended when the king died of something rather unpleasant in Tunisia during the summer of 1270. There were further attempts to try and raise Crusades but, quite frankly, everyone was so fed up with continually sailing across treacherous seas, climbing over torturous mountain passes, and trekking across searing deserts (before having to face the dreaded foe), that they began to hesitate. In the end, all that remained were a bunch of dusty old crusader churches, a few battered castles, a history full of tall tales, and a lot of ill will between major religions.

KNIGHTS OF ALL KINDS

You might have heard people talk about the Knights Templars or the Knights Hospitalers. I'll try to explain what they were and to throw in a few of the other knighty types for good measure.

The Knights Templars

These were a splendid bunch of knights who ranked somewhere between things godly and things military. They were recognized wherever they went by their brilliant white tabards (garment worn over armor) sporting big red crosses.

By the Way

The crosses worn by the Templars were Maltese crosses, not quite the same as the Christian crosses worn by Richard the Lion-Hearted (on his cloak) or the crusaders (over their breastplates).

The Templars began as a little gang of eight knights led by the Burgundian knight Hugh de Payens and his friend André de Montbard. They acted as guides and protectors to the Christian pilgrims passing through hostile lands on their way to Jerusalem. Up until the middle of the eleventh century, the Muslims, who held Jerusalem, had allowed Christian pilgrims to visit. When a different bunch of Muslims (Turkish ones) took over, they went out of their way to attack and rob the pilgrims on the way there. The Muslims regarded the pilgrims as a gift from God . . . and then stopped them from coming altogether. This made the knights very angry indeed. By the time the First Crusade was under way, these guys decided to become a religious order, calling themselves the Poor Knights of the Temple of Solomon (or the Knights Templars for short). They were first recognized at the Council of Troyes (and given permission to wear their famous red crosses) by the church's Bernard of Clairvaux. (He did so well, by the way, that he went on to be a saint.)

Bernard was the most important churchman of the time. He had preached in favor of the Second Crusade and had coaxed many knights to join. Bernard liked the idea of knights who were religious rather than just out for what they could get. He granted them their rule (called The Rule) in 1128. Gifts and money poured in to support these noble fellows. Soon most major cities had recruitment centers where the starter-knights from the best families in Europe went to train.

Sworn to a life of poverty, chastity, and obedience, the Knights Templars became the most dedicated, scariest soldiers and would fight anywhere they were required. They became so powerful that they eventually chose which of the king's orders they would obey. At their height, there were 20,000 Knights Templars as well as their sergeants, chaplains, and servants. They owned massive estates from Denmark and the Orkney Islands in the north, to Italy and Spain in the south.

The Knights Templars became most famous for defending the Christian enclave of Jerusalem even though they did fall out big-time with their rivals the Knights Hospitalers. To say "fall out" was no exaggeration—they hated each other with a passion. In the end, they were fighting each other in the streets.

After the Crusades, most of the ordinary crusaders went home. The job of keeping the Turks and the Egyptians at bay fell to the Templars and the Hospitalers. Those mighty crusader castles that stretch all the way through Turkey and southern Europe were built during this period. Because they actually lived in the Holy Land, the Templars often looked at things differently than the part-time crusaders who, let's face it, only turned up briefly to fight the Muslims and grab as much money as they could get their hands on.

After the capture of ancient seaport of Acre (later renamed Akko) in 1291, the rest of the kingdom of Jerusalem was lost, and the Templars withdrew to their European operations. These operations involved international trade, banking, and diplomacy at which they were so brilliant that they soon became ludicrously wealthy (so much for their vows of poverty). They even bought a huge fleet of highly maneuverable warships (complete with battering rams) so that they could transport pilgrims, troops, and horses. They made huge profits partly due to the fact that they had long ago been given exemption from taxes. Also, they didn't have to answer to any law but God's (which was a big disappointment for everyone else). As is usually the case, jealousy made them very unpopular.

By the Way

Did you know that the Knights Templars were responsible for bringing the idea of mouth-to-mouth resuscitation, the telescope, and the personal check to Europe from the Holy Land? The long-distance traveler could carry a kind of Templars' credit card. It not only saved the person from carrying cash but meant that he or she could use it wherever the traveler found a Templar in residence.

So the Knights Templars became richer and richer and more and more powerful until Friday the 13th⋆ in October of 1307. King Philip IV of France, who was getting exceedingly hot under the crown, decided to accuse them of heresy (disagreeing with the teachings of the church).

⋆ *Unlucky for some*

This decision revealed Philip's sour grapes—he'd been refused admission to the order when he was a young man. Philip demanded to have all the Knights Templars in France arrested and the order promptly abolished. The knights were then tortured so badly that they admitted to a bunch of crimes they didn't commit. For punishment, they were burned slowly. The Templars' property was handed over to the Hospitalers who were waiting in the wings with huge grins on their greedy faces. The pope then ordered that similar persecution of the Templars happen in every country in which the Templars owned property.

By the Way

It is thought that seventeen Templar ships, loaded with the hoard of treasure that had been stored in Paris Temple 29, left from various French ports. The treasure was never seen again. If you want to know where it is, send me a fiver, and I'll tell you.

The Knights of Saint John of Jerusalem— or the Knights Hospitalers

The Hospitalers were the other great order of religious knights who gradually got more and more into fighting for a living. Like the Templars, their main job was to guard, guide, and comfort the weary pilgrims on their way to and from Jerusalem. In 1112 their monastery (or hospital) not only held all of them but up to 2,000 guests (sounds more like a hotel than a hospital!). The Hospitalers wore black outfits with white crosses and built fabulous castles that became hospitals for old or sick knights, as well as barracks for their soldiers.

Acre fell to the Muslims in 1291, so the Hospitalers settled on the island of Cyprus to regroup. Then they went into the profitable shipping business, providing the Christian countries with supplies from Asia while keeping down pirates in the Mediterranean. In 1307 they bought the Greek island of Rhodes and made it their fortified headquarters (you can still see their castles on the island). The Muslims didn't like having a Christian stronghold so close to their lands and attacked them (unsuccessfully) in 1435.

After the Turks sacked Constantinople in 1453, the Hospitalers became the last Christians left in the Middle East, a fact that made life even trickier for them. They were attacked several times again and were finally beaten in 1522 by the massive army of the Turkish sultan, Süleyman the Magnificent. The victors, however, let the Hospitalers leave the island with their lives as a mark of respect for their loony bravery.

Emperor Charles V thought the Hospitalers were really cool. So, he gave them the island of Malta, which was a good deal, all things considered. Wouldn't you know, that blasted Süleyman (at the age of seventy) tried again. The amazing Knights Hospitalers totaled only 700 knights and 1,500 men.

Yet, they managed to hold off the full might of the Turkish Empire and became legendary heroes for their trouble.

By the Way

The Knights Hospitalers, established in 1100 in England, survived until 1540, when Henry VIII dissolved the group. Queen Victoria, for some reason, reinstated them in 1888. The Knights Templars and the Knights Hospitalers still exist but only as clubs (just like the Freemasons) patronized by businesspeople.

BYE DARLING—LOVE TO THE OTHER KNIGHTS

Teutonic Knights of the Virgin Mary

Yet another bunch of religious knuts—sorry—knights, the Teutonic Knights of the Virgin Mary followed vows of poverty, chastity, and obedience. This bunch began after the fall of ancient Acre and only concerned themselves with protecting German pilgrims. They were known by their white tunic with a black cross (confusing or what?). In the thirteenth century, they switched from protecting people to killing them and eventually ruled all the land between the Vistula River and Memel (which later become Klaipėda, Lithuania). (Try to visit their string of fantastic castles.) It's almost funny, but, being Christians themselves, they were nearly destroyed by Christian Polish and Lithuanian forces in 1410. The poor Teutonic Knights limped on until Napoleon finally grabbed them and seized all of their remaining worldly goods.

Odd Knights and Knightesses

Through the ages, there have been all kinds of weird and wonderful societies of knights. These societies included the Orders of Dog and Cock, the Palm and Alligator, the Fools—I'm not making these up—the Bee, the Broom Flowers, the Slaves of Virtue, the Angelic Knights, the Dove of Castile, etc., as well as a few female orders.

KNIGHT EQUIPMENT

One of the troubles with having pointy things like lances and swords stabbed at you or sharp things like arrows and bolts fired at you is that your skin isn't really designed to withstand it. Early on, people discovered that it might be a smart idea to put something tougher between their bodies and whatever it was that whomever it was was trying to puncture them with.

The trouble with wearing anything hard, unfortunately, is that it's usually inflexible and reduces the wearer's ability to run around (or away!). Something had to be found that was both bendy and tough at the same time. The answer was one of those things that seems obvious now—like the wheel (or the microchip, if you're a genius)—but was nothing less than inspired when first thought of.

Chain Mail and Helmets

Until the end of the eleventh century, your average knight went into battle dressed from head to knee in a sort of long, hooded dress (called a hauberk) made of little joined iron rings—like knitted metal. These rings were either punched out of a sheet of iron or handmade out of wire with the ends flattened. All in all, there were at least a 100,000 rings in the average garment. The whole thing weighed about twenty-six pounds. On top of the hood the knight wore a conical (and sometimes

IS IT A LITTLE HEAVY DEAR?

comical) metal helmet or helm with a part sticking down the front to protect his nose. For added protection, he carried a huge shield shaped like a kite.

By the Way

The shield was made big enough to enable a knight to drag a wounded friend on it if necessary.

Experts are continually astonished by the fact that, despite the European knights' contact with the heavily, cleverly armored Turkish and Byzantine soldiers during the Crusades, very few of their techniques rubbed off on the knights. The English and French knights copied the idea of wearing a heavily padded and quilted undergarment (called a gambeson) underneath their chain mail and a plain linen surcoat (outer coat) over it. They also adopted the use of chain mail gloves and boots, which were laced on to the arms and legs.

By the twelfth century, things had changed a lot. Instead of the pointy helmet that had replaced the conical sort, the knight went back to a cylindrical helmet, only this time much bigger (like a small upturned garbage can). This headgear was so heavy that it was designed to rest on the wearer's shoulders. For the first time, the helmet covered the whole face, with slits for the eyes and holes down the front for speaking (and presumably breathing). Later on these helmets (also called helms) sported ornaments—anything from plumes or fans to large scary horns—and could have movable visors. The headgear being so cumbersome, any knight with any sense only put it on at the last minute.

By the Way

The cry "helms on," was often the last cry heard before a medieval brawl commenced. I expect "run for it" could have been the second.

By Another Way

The trouble with the one-piece helmets was that, if the wearer received a blow, they could easily swivel around, moving the eye-slits away from the knight's vision. Made completely blind, the poor knight was then at a disadvantage in the old battle scenario.

Who's Who?

Next they padded the undergarment with leather after boiling it to make it harder. The linen surcoat began to carry an identifying coat of arms so that the soldiers could identify each other during a rumble, preventing the possibility of harming someone on their own side. These identification symbols were the beginning of heraldry.

Real Armor

The first real plate armor was worn under the outer garments as extra protection (chilly or what?). Chain gloves only got places for fingers by the end of the twelfth century. By the beginning of the fourteenth century, metal plates appeared everywhere, protecting the front of the knees, the shins, the arms, the elbows, and the shoulders. Keep in mind, a skillful swordsman could still find places to poke his blade, like under the arms, in the neck, or between the legs (ouch!). Later they developed little round steel discs called *basagews* purely to protect those vulnerable little places.

By the mid-fourteenth century, knights began to look how we imagine them now. They wore a fifty-fifty combination of mail and plate armor with a big sheet of shiny, shaped iron strapped over the chest. A shorter tunic that tied at the sides covered this chest plate. The knight's personal coat of arms decorated the front. As a knight's protection improved, by the way, his shield got smaller . . . for fairly obvious reasons.* So by this point his shield wasn't much bigger than a meal tray.

Fully Canned

This was about as far as it went for the English knights. They sensibly realized that they had reached a certain balance between protection and being able to move—the more you had, the less you could, so to speak! Otherwise they might as well have been wheeled out in a giant iron box with a hole in the front for their sword. (I've heard of worse ideas!)

* *Oh, okay, I'll tell you: they didn't need a big shield when body armor was working so well.*

The thick armor with pointed helmets and spikes on the elbows and shoulders was less practical. Mostly made and worn by Italians, French, or Germans, the style was often for purely ceremonial wear. The snout-faced helmets called basinets were designed to give the wearers a very scary and very hard appearance.

By the Way

Although meant to protect, armor caused many fatalities. The middle-aged knights often died of heart failure on the battlefield, before they even got near the enemy. On hot summer days (especially likely in the Middle East), the poor metallic guys could literally roast. This happened to Edward of York just before the Battle of Agincourt in France, although the temperature inside his suit probably owed a lot to his fatness as well.

The other slight problem that the armored knight had to contend with occurred during thunderstorms—not from rust, as you might imagine, but from lightning. Many a knight and his horse were struck at the same time. At the battles of Crécy and Poitiers in France, more knights lost their lives from lightning strikes than from the best efforts of the enemy.

How Heavy?

It is widely believed that a full harness* of armor weighed so much that the wearers could hardly move. But in the wonderful *Dictionary of Chivalry*, Grant Uden tells a different story. He suggests that the weight depended on how well it was made. The finest armor fit like a second skin. To achieve this quality, armorers employed hammermen to beat out the metal, millmen to polish it, and locksmiths to make the fastenings and hinges. If the guys making the arms couldn't actually meet their customers (overseas battle commitments, etc.), elaborate measurements or even actual models of their limbs were sent from far and wide.

---

* *It's very uncool, apparently, if you ever meet a knight, to call his gear a "suit" of armor.*

Did you know, for instance, that:

1. A full harness in the fifteenth century weighed less than the equipment that foot soldiers had to wear in World War I?

2. The English king Edward I could leap into the saddle—without stirrups—in full armor?

3. Tests in America recently showed that these days a healthy young man in well-fitting armor could still move athletically, jump on a horse, and dismount without any help?

How Much?

If you are anything like me, you'll probably be more interested in what all this equipment cost. The total is difficult to find out, as many kings and landed gentry had their own personal armorers. But the majority didn't, and they would have had to buy the stuff like anyone else. Not, however, off the shelf, but specially tailored to fit their bodies—exactly.

A realistic figure, having spoken to various experts in the field, is that a full set of armor, not including anything you might spend on horses and weapons, would probably cost you the price of a new Ferrari (on average costing about $215,000, in case you don't have one). This, as you might imagine, really would sort out the men from the boys.

Where?

As I said earlier, people like kings and dukes probably had their own armorers who lived in their castles. Anyone else who wanted a harness (remember it's not a suit!), however, had to have them made by a private armorer. These shops were usually located in the East End of London and in other big cities throughout Europe. In 1322 anyone who wanted to make arms and armor had to belong to a guild. That guild, called the Armourers Company, still exists today.

By the Way

If you're after a new harness of armor, a chain mail vest, or a new sword—worry not. If you write to the Royal Armoury Museum in Leeds, England, they'll fix you up with something right away.

THINGS TO FIGHT WITH

Knights of old had a range of nasty things to hit and stab each other with. Here are a few of the best they used and also some of the weapons used by other people on the knights.

Battle-Ax

A terrible weapon if you happen to be on the receiving end. This ax had a perfectly balanced handle. Fighters swung it wildly around their heads, using both hands. Knights often used the battle-ax in hand-to-hand combat when knocked off their horses.

Dagger

More like a short sword, a dagger was anything up to two feet long, double edged, and sharp as a razor. The dagger began life (and also ended it!!) in the early Middle Ages.

Falchion

A type of sword used by knights and foot soldiers throughout the Middle Ages. Some widened considerably toward the point and had one convex cutting edge.

Fork

More popular with foot soldiers than knights, as they were often used to pull the knights off of their horses. The fork had three sharp prongs with hooks on the end to grip its victim.

Glaive

A horrible-looking weapon that was basically a curved sword stuck on the end of a long pole.

Gisarme

Again not popular with knights, as they were used by foot soldiers to attack them. Gisarmes were a cross between a pike and a scythe—very unpleasant. Used in great swinging circles.

Halberd

A long-handled ax, sometimes six feet in length, with a sharp spike on the end. Often used like a can opener against a fully canned (covered) knight.

Lance

The main weapon of the knight both in battle and at jousts (fighting contests). For years it was simply a sharpened pole, over twelve feet in length, tipped with metal. Sometimes a special bracket was fitted to the breastplate of the armor so as to take the butt of the lance and therefore the impact. Later lances had a "vamplate," a metal disc near the holding end specifically designed to protect the hands.

Mace

The most common sort of mace was the one with a spiked iron ball on the end of a pole. If one of these struck you, you'd certainly know about it, as it was capable of doing terrible damage. Some maces, called flails, were even more unpleasant. They had a spiky part that attached to a chain that attached to a handle. This meant that it could be swung around at great speed and could catch the opponent unaware.

Main-Gauche

From the French meaning left hand, this was a dangerous little dagger held in the left hand to parry blows while the other hand was busy with the big, real sword.

Partisan

Another kind of halberd or pike, with a double-edged tapering blade on the end of a long pole. It was generally regarded as the knight's worst enemy.

Poleax

Often used by knights, the six-foot-long poleax did several jobs. It had a cutting edge, a hammerhead, and a sharp spike on the end.

Rapier

Slim pointy sword used in hand-to-hand combat
that was used to pierce the opponent rather
than cut him.

Scimitar

Dangerous, single-edged, curved sword that
broadened toward the point, and was a favorite
weapon of the Turks.

Two-Handed or Giant Sword

Massive sword that was so heavy it could only be
held in two hands. Used in long sweeps,
this five- to six-foot-long weapon could
take a limb off (no trouble)—even if said
limb wore armor.

War Hammer

Guaranteed to cause quite a headache if it caught your
helmet. The war hammer resembles the sort of hammer
your dad or mom uses but much bigger, and it's
on the end of a pole with a spike coming out of
the top.

A KNIGHT'S HOME
IS HIS CASTLE

If you want to know about knights, you'll probably also need to know about castles. I mean, you couldn't really imagine a proud knight in full battle armor, astride a magnificent charger pulling up outside a hut. He'd look silly (and what would the neighbors say!). Most English castles were built in those rough, tough days around the twelfth century, when just about everybody was fighting everybody. It became necessary, therefore, for gentlemen to build their homes in such a style as to keep out other gentlemen. The peasants' homes, of course, didn't matter nearly as much, because a) nobody really wanted their homes, and b) nobody really cared about what happened to peasants.

Le Castle

The idea of castles as we know them came from France, where the great lords had been building them for centuries. Records show that back in 864, the old smoothy, Charles the

Bald of France, grumpily decreed that nobody could build a castle without his say-so (so there!). This was really annoying, because castles were already an integral part of the feudal system, acting as the focal point of a knight's fief. In return for the peasants sweating their guts out to feed and, if picked, fight for the knight, that knight had to provide a great big safe house for them to scurry into if ever chased.

All Fall Down

Although castles really began in France, it soon became clear that the Norman masons weren't always that brilliant with tall structures. These masons came to England from what is now a part of France in 1066, when a Norman, William the Conqueror, . . . um conquered . . . England. Many of the great towers the Normans built in England simply fell down due to their scrawny foundations. Actually to be fair, the poor Normans only had Saxon labor to work with, and these early Brits were awful at building anything bigger than a hut.

Where?

Once a knight or baron decided to build a new castle, he had to determine where to put the darn thing. The answer was usually pretty obvious—on top of something—preferably on a large hill. The height advantage meant that your watchmen could see anyone coming from miles around and give you time to prepare. Plus, if your new visitors were less than friendly, they were usually so exhausted by the time they reached the outer walls that they couldn't do much anyway.

They also usually built castles very close to rivers. This location made the delivery of building materials (and water) much easier. Very few roads existed in those days (and those that did were usually Roman, worn out, and seldom going anywhere you wanted to go!).

By the Way

By the middle of the eleventh century, castle builders decided that if there wasn't a natural hill near where they wanted their structure, they'd order the poor long-suffering peasants to make one, with their bare hands, and call it a motte. There are lots of these mottes, looking like overgrown molehills, all over Britain.

Made of What?

Once he chose (or made) a site, Mr. Knight had to decide what to build his castle out of. Just like the three little pigs, they found out that big bad enemies have little trouble attacking anything less substantial than stone. A couple of flaming arrows in a wooden castle and the game was up—roast pork for all! That's why none of the earlier castles, built out of wood, still stand. But in those days, England was mostly forest. Wood was free and there for the taking. To get around the fire problem, early timber-built castles often had really high, really wide, arrow-proof stone walls surrounding them.

What Sort of Castle?

There were two main types of castle in those days. Those with a keep had a big central building that could usually defend itself. Those without a keep simply relied on the strength of the outer walls or palisades. Your top-of-the-line castle came fully loaded with a great big keep and huge surrounding walls and towers, within which all the other outbuildings were built. The keep, by the way, was where all the peasants ran when there was trouble coming.

One Way Out!

Early castles were usually built with only one way to get out! This silly idea usually meant that attackers could simply hang around the front door as long as they liked, until the occupants needed to come out. Later castle designers realized this and made little concealed doorways (called posterns) at the back, so that if things got tricky the occupants could sneak away one at a time. Sometimes they even dug secret tunnels that came up in the fresh air as far away as they could dig.

Most good castles had a wide ditch or moat around them—the wider the better—filled with water. Those inside could lower and raise a drawbridge so that no one could get to them without a severe soaking.

Starting Off

First you ordered your peasant workers to haul up huge amounts of timber or stones to the top of the motte they just made. These materials were often brought upriver on barges and unloaded as near as possible to the site. Castles usually had to be built in a hurry because knights (especially Norman knights) expected people to attack every five minutes (which they often did). But what did these massive edifices cost?

Well, if the records from 1296 of the building of Beaumaris Castle in Gwynedd, Wales, are anything to go by—they cost an absolute fortune.

For a start, they had over 100 carts and thirty boats running to and fro bringing the stone and the wood (for the temporary buildings that the workcrews lived in). On-site, over 1,000 skilled carpenters, plasterers, and stonemasons, as well as 2,000 minor workers, labored.

These workers needed protection from attackers. For this they employed 10 watchmen, 20 crossbowmen, and 100 infantrymen. The construction of Beaumaris Castle went on for thirteen years and was only half-finished when the best castle builder of the time, James of St. George, died. And that's nothing. Caernarvon Castle, also in Wales, was started in 1283 and was eventually finished (almost) in 1327—forty-four years later.

By the Way

James was one of the most highly regarded architects and engineers of the time, earning the equivalent of $92,000 a year—a fortune for the time.

Early Castles

In the very beginning, barons, their families, servants, pets, and sometimes even farm animals all lived in one great, nifty hall. When the Normans came, however, they weren't too eager to share with livestock (or was it the other way around?). They moved the dirty beasts into the bailey (the part between the main house and the outside wall). The main hall (a room raised off the ground and called the dais) was full of tables and benches, draped with animal skins, and decorated with curtains and colorful tapestries. A kitchen, separate from the main hall, kept the stray sparks of the massive open cooking fires from setting the whole structure ablaze (which tended to ruin mealtimes). In the main hall, the fire burned in the middle of the room, as far from the walls as possible (for obvious reasons). Smoke escaped through a little hole in the roof covered by its own little roof, or louver, to stop the rain from getting in.

Real Castles

But what about those castles you see in picture books, with battlements and little pointy flags on the turrets? These began to appear in the twelfth century, and many still stand, admittedly past their prime. The inspiration for these wonderful buildings, particularly the pointy Gothic style, almost certainly came to Europe via the crusaders. They saw the fabulous fortresses and temples of the Middle East and even brought back prisoners who knew how to build them.

By the Way

One such prisoner, a guy called Lalys, designed Neath Abbey in southern Wales and became Henry I's favorite architect.

THAT MIGHT CATCH ON

By Another Way

Even for building a simple garage these days, the architect produces many boring technical drawings that conform with local building regulations. The final plans have to be approved by the local government's planning department before starting construction. After the garage is finished, the building inspector comes around and passes the work. In those days, because no drawings have ever been found, it seems obvious that they simply scratched out the design in the dirt and got to work. Most of these castles still stood for hundreds of years. Does that tell us something?

The derelict castle at Orford in eastern England, which was started in 1165, is typical of those built at that time. It was originally located beside a harbor (which has since dried up). The main keep is circular inside but outside has three massive square towers protecting it and holding it up. Between these, on the outside, there were originally crenellated fighting decks.

There were storerooms and pantries on the ground level. The area below them included dungeons and sometimes the dreaded oubliette (from the French *oublier*—to forget). Captors threw the poor victim into this hole in the ground and sort of—well—forgot them. Above the storerooms sat a massive round main hall with beautifully painted beams soaring to a point high above the floor. Above that, suites of rooms contained a small kitchen for reheating meals, making sauces, and roasting and smoking small joints of meat. They did all of the main cooking in the timber kitchens between the keep and the outer walls.

The bedrooms were set into the turrets adjoining the main structure, so the occupants could see out of the windows. At the very top, a flat roof with the guards' quarters and watchtower kept inhabitants abreast of any exterior developments. Just below, a huge cistern (well) contained water for the whole castle. If you're wondering about bathrooms, yes, they did have them, but they were not as good as those you have at home (I hope). They simply consisted of sloped, interconnecting channels that ran from top to bottom, dropping down into a pit so deep that it never needed emptying. (Better than the bushes, I suppose.)

The average medieval castle's outer walls sheltered many assorted buildings: chambers for the clergy, offices for the scribes, and counting-houses for the castle's finance managers. There were closets for the knight and his lady's clothes, dairies to make butter and cheese, carpentry shops for repairs, aviaries for birds (both for singing and eating), and covered walkways to keep the food dry as it traveled from the kitchen to the dining hall. There was a chapel in which to pray, a safe room in which to store all the gold and silver (and cash taken off the tenants), a special room in which to keep all the valuable deeds, an armory for storing all the weapons, stables for the horses, a laundry . . . pause for breath . . . for the washing, wine cellars to store the booze, and a cool place for brewing beer. In fact, the walls practically contained a small town.

Approach with Caution

The main door at the front of the keep had a gigantic portcullis (barred gate) that could be raised and lowered from above. Just above the archway leading to this portcullis was usually a murder hole—a tricky, if somewhat obvious, device that was simply a hole in the ceiling through which rocks, arrows, hot  oil, rotten eggs, or something even worse could be dropped on unwanted visitors (like insurance salespeople).

Breaking and Entering

However fortified a castle might be, it didn't stop people from trying to break in or beat the occupants into submission. One standard way, digging underneath the castle to undermine the structure, happened at Rochester Castle, near London, in the twelfth century.

King John busied himself with laying siege to a bunch of knights he didn't like. He got his diggers to dig right under the southeastern corner of the building. Then they stuffed the tunnel with straw soaked in pig fat (roast pork yet again) and lit them. The huge fire caused the very foundations of the building to give way and brought down the massive corner turret. The king's men then rushed in and forced the residents back into the keep, where, after eating their horses, they eventually surrendered due to starvation.

This became such a common way of attacking a castle that the original builders eventually created a solution. They made a network of passages underneath so that the residents could locate any new passages and shoo the interlopers away or smoke them out. Anyone with any real sense, however, built their castle on rock, which solved the problem nicely.

By the Way

To get some idea of the scale of some of these operations, during the attack on the fortress of Acre in 1291, 1,000 engineers and miners attacked the eleven outer towers at the same time.

Over the Top

If this method didn't work, attackers could try one of the other ways of storming a castle. Best of all were the massive war machines. The idea for these overgrown catapults called mangonels originally came from ancient Greece. They were powered by twisted animal skins and sinews that acted like giant rubber bands. There were also ballistae, giant crossbows, that fired huge arrows or rocks horizontally. The rocks they fired would crack the outer surface of the castle walls. This strategy allowed the attackers to use picks and shovels to tear away the rubble and loose stones that filled the two outer skins of the average castle wall. While they scraped, of course, the defenders felt free to pour hot oil or tip rocks onto them—great fun. Eventually the workers wised up and wheeled in a penthouse, a portable wooden shelter under which they could work away to their hearts' content.

French Machines

Later, new stone-throwing machines from France, called trebuchets, were developed, powered by twisted skins and ultraspringy green wood. These worked by using counterweights. The machines came small enough for one man to fire or so enormous (up to fifty feet in length) that it took teams of oxen to get them into position and more than twenty men to operate.

These catapulting devices were so big and powerful that they could've thrown a grand piano (if they'd had them). Both sides, in and out of the castle, had these machines. Oftentimes, they recycled the opponent's missiles and sent them flying back. Take that!

By the Way

It was common to throw the stinky carcasses of dead sheep or horses over the walls in hopes of spreading disease among the inhabitants. Mean or what?

By Another Way

Attackers sometimes used Greek fire, a lethal mixture of naphtha, quicklime, and sulfur. When lit and catapulted in earthenware pots, the goo would stick to whatever it came in contact with. This could be very unpleasant. If thrown on water, it would burn even more fiercely because of the quicklime.

Gunsmoke

By the early fourteenth century, everyone was talking about a new super-duper weapon. The idea supposedly came from China. Early drawings show what looks like a large vase tipped on its side with a massive arrow flying from its neck. At the back of the vase was a little armored guy holding a lighted torch to a little hole. No prizes for guessing that this was an early cannon, powered by gunpowder.

The recipe for gunpowder first appeared in England in a coded note from Roger Bacon, a philosopher, scientist, and Franciscan monk, in 1260. It must be said, however, that despite the early cannons' frightening bang, they were slow to load, had a short range, and were no match for the skilled longbowmen in early battle trials.

Blow the Walls Down

If the assailants could reach the castle door or a flat piece of wall, they used enormous battering rams—huge tree trunks with metal ends, set into frames, and mounted on rollers. Untreated (and smelly) animal skins covered the rams to protect the pushers from being hit and set afire by flaming missiles from above. Sometimes the defenders lowered straw mattresses to cushion the blows from the ram or huge hooks on chains to try to pull the thing out of the way.

Siege Towers

As well as huge ladders for scaling the walls, the attackers built lofty towers the same height as the walls. They would then flatten the land up to the walls and wheel the ladders into place so that the soldiers could throw bridges across onto the battlements. The towers, often several stories high, were usually covered in waterlogged animal skins to snuff out flaming arrows.

Siege Time

All that tunneling and shooting and ramming and stuff worked well, but it often seemed like very hard, unnecessary work. It was much easier to surround a castle, with the knight and his company locked safely inside, cut off their supplies and communications, and simply sit it out. In fact, in the 1100s, the English king Stephen spent most of his reign lounging around outside of various castles waiting for the people inside to come out with their hands up. These sieges went on for months or, on rare occasions, years. They only ended when those inside had eaten everything possible (including each other) and drunk everything possible (yes, even that!!!). Sometimes, if a well ran dry or the water supply was cut off, the inmates resorted to drinking the vast wine supplies of the castle's cellars. They not only drank it, they used it to cook and even put out fires with it, when really desperate. A dreadful waste to me.

WHERE'S CHARLIE?

WE HAD HIM YESTERDAY

Food Alert!

The famous siege of Rouen in France by England's Henry V went on from July 29, 1418, to January 13, 1419. By Christmas the inhabitants had run out of food completely. Having eaten all their supplies, only horses, dogs, cats, mice, and the occasional rat remained. Those who could still stand upright were paraded along the battlements to try to make the English think that everything was still okay. So as not to have to share, the poorer townsfolk (men, women, and children) were shoved outside the town gates and told they had to fend for themselves. Thus, they revealed the real situation anyway. It was the old good news/bad news scenario yet again. England's kind king took pity on them and gave them food and water. But, unfortunately, he wouldn't let them in his camp. Most died from the freezing cold and damp.

Most of the time, those doing the sieging got a pleasant break, waiting around for those inside to give in. Sometimes they had feasts and tournaments to pass the time. Even those outside, however, had trouble getting food and supplies themselves. This posed a problem, especially if those inside had realized that they were due for a siege and stocked up. It was not unusual, therefore, to have a scenario where the siegers, starving to death, threw up their hands and retreated home.

End Note

Toward the end of the Middle Ages, most people began to behave themselves. The need for massive stone-built fortifications, towers, and moats reduced considerably. The age of the castle was soon finished.

FORGET THIS FOR A GAME OF SOLDIERS!

TOURNAMENTS

If you think knights liked hunting, feasting, and breaking into each other's castles, they liked tournaments even more. Nothing (apart from maybe the Crusades) was better designed to show off what they stood for than these elaborate medieval festivals. A young knight could display bravery, agility, mercy, and fair play while seeking employment with the lords who were always on the lookout for new talent. Not only that, it provided a poor man a way to gain a fortune, lands, and respect. Best of all, it was a chance to show off in front of the local ladies and compete for their favors.

If hunting was unpopular with the church, tournaments were the ultimate no-no. They were seen as just a lightly hidden training ground for war. Even Henry II forbade them because they led to the shocking waste of young lives. And shocking it often was: William Marshal, a knight who fought twice a month when young, claimed that in 1240 between sixty and eighty contestants were slaughtered in a frenzy of killing at one single tournament.

By the Way

After one famous victory, poor Will had to resort to the blacksmith's shop to have his head pried out of his helmet.

HE REALLY SHOULD KEEP HIS HELMET ON!

King Richard the Lion-Hearted wasn't as worried about the loss of life. He saw it as a way of drumming up money for his Crusades. He licensed five sites called steads for the tournaments to take place. To take part, a combatant had to pay a fee in advance according to his rank.

That was in the early days, however, when tournaments were not much less than free-for-alls with posses of knights from various towns or cities attacking each other in fearsome battles. The object was usually to take as many prisoners as possible and to ransom them back to their families.

All for One

As tournaments developed, they became less like brawls between rival gangs and more like individual campaigns for aspiring young knights. In fact, these guys wandered the countryside, like prizefighters or gunslingers, looking for tournaments to show off their skills, earn huge amounts of cash, and maybe even get their chain-mailed mitts on the lord's prettiest daughter. Some knights became completely addicted to tournaments, mortgaging their estates and livestock even when it led to eventual bankruptcy and ruin. Sure the big prize could set you up for life, but if you lost and weren't killed, you could expect to lose your horse, your armor, and possibly your freedom. Individual knights, beaten fairly and squarely in a joust, often ended up being ransomed by their victor—imagine that!

Despite the vibrant color, music, feasting, and carnival atmosphere, however, tournaments were still basically savage affairs. Many healthy young warriors ended their days bleeding to death on the grass in front of a rapturous audience. They fought like gladiators in Roman times except then it was sand, not grass.

Going Soft

Later on, to curb the fatalities, weapons were blunted and barriers were put between the jousters to stop them from crashing into one another. Even so, when tournaments had become merely stylized parodies of themselves, occasionally lances still penetrated visors and gave the occupant more than a headache. More than that, if tempers got lost, blunted weapons couldn't save the combatants from doing each other in. At one tournament in France in 1273, the duke of Burgundy really lost it. He seized England's king Edward I around the neck to pull him off of his horse and strangle him. Eddie galloped off, dangling the desperate duke behind him. Suddenly foot soldiers on both sides dashed to support their leaders, and both sides fired their crossbows at each other—good game! Many people were killed at what became the Battle of Châlons.

Trouble at Home

All this tournamenting was fine but it often led to the knights neglecting their lands back home. At one point it became difficult for a king to raise an army to kill his enemies with, as there were so many knights busy killing each other—for fun.

Later Tournaments

Toward the end of the Middle Ages, tournaments changed from bloody battlegrounds to rather theatrical displays of wealth, breeding, and athletic skills. Impoverished knights from not-very-good families found it impossible to succeed, because the cost of armor and other necessary equipment (horses, etc.) was becoming extraordinary. Hand-to-hand fighting to the death became practically a thing of the past. Jousting, with all the new safety rules and regulations, became more popular. Scoring counted how many times and where a knight struck his opponent. A blow to the helmet scored well, but if a knight actually managed to knock his opponent off his horse, that knight hit the jackpot big time.

Costs

So what did it all cost? Answer—a lot! One knight, who went by the name of William de la Zouche, paid well over the equivalent of $45,000 to King Edward III's armorer, John Skelton. The amount bought him gold and silver foil, silk fringes, and all the pieces needed to decorate the harnesses, banners, crests, and fabrics for himself and his horse. That cost didn't include his actual armor, the total of which I've already given you some idea.

GOOD KNIGHTS

Although most of the knights of the Middle Ages received bad press, others became famous for their heroism and bravery. Here are my favorites:

Saladin

Saladin, the sultan of Egypt and Syria in the 1100s, was the most feared enemy of the crusaders. Small, modest, and scholarly, he was obviously not a real knight. Most reporters of the time, however, claimed he possessed the knightly qualities that many of the so-called Christians lacked. He was known for amazing acts of generosity and true chivalry.

One act of kindness occurred with the flamboyant Richard the Lion-hearted. When Saladin heard that Richard was dying of a fever in his tent, Saladin sent fresh peaches and pears and even snow from the peak of Mount Hermon to help cool him down. Another time, when Richard had parted company with his horse in battle, the sultan sent him a few replacements. Poor Saladin died at the age of fifty-four, worn out by continual fighting.

Sir William Longsword

Another knight, twenty-seven-year-old Sir William Longsword became more famous for his spectacular death at El Mansûra, Egypt, than anything else. In 1250 the Christian knights were getting a licking from the Egyptian Muslim army. It had come down to hand-to-hand fighting in the streets of the city. The brave Sir William and his standard-bearer (the person who carries the banner of a knight) Sir Richard de Guise were getting the worst of it. Richard had already lost his hand and yet continued to hold the banner up with his brand-new stump. Then the Muslims, who couldn't seem to get Sir William out of his saddle, sliced off his left foot. This annoyed the young knight, so he got down from the saddle and, supporting himself on another friend, Richard of Ascalon, continued fighting on the other leg. Then another sword swipe took care of his right arm, which was inconvenient, to say the least. Now without any support at all, he hopped into the attack once more, grasping his sword in his other hand. It was promptly lopped off, too. Oh dear, things were now looking pretty tricky for the poor handless, armless, and one-footed warrior. It wasn't long before he tipped over and the Muslims attacked until there was hardly anything recognizable left of poor Willie. While this was happening, Richard of Ascalon had joined his master to try to save him but, as you might imagine, he suffered the same fate.

John FitzThomas, Earl of Kildare

During the Scottish wars, one of Edward I's knights, John, always carried the livery of a chained monkey on his crest. Here's why. When he was a little kid in the castle in Woodstock, Ireland, a bad fire broke out. So bad that with all the rushing around no one thought to get little Johnny until it seemed too late. At the end of the night, when they finally got to the poor toddler's bedroom, it was burned to cinders. The end of the knight? No . . . just as his family was tearing their hair out with grief, they heard a strange noise coming from high on the battlements. It was

the family's pet monkey (who was usually chained up), with the baby John in its arms. When he grew up and became a knight (the baby, not the monkey), Sir John put a picture of the monkey on his crest in gratitude.

Sir Giles d'Argentine

Sir Giles was probably the most famous knight in the Battle of Bannockburn (1314), at which the English, under Edward II, were shown where to get off by Robert the Bruce. (What is a Bruce?) With the archers cut into little pieces and the cavalry up to their necks in the peat bogs, the English king was dragged from the fun by a company of his most trusty knights. They galloped off to bring him to safety. Out of harm's reach, the brave (if not stupid) Sir Giles pulled up his horse and cried, "I am not of custom to fly; nor shall I do so now. God keep you!" With that he charged back toward the battle and certain death. Silly man!

Sir James Douglas the Good

After the death of King Robert the Bruce in 1329, Scottish knight Sir Douglas was given his leader's heart in a silver casket. He was asked to take it to the Holy Land, so that Robert I could carry out his crusader's vow (to lead the army to get the Holy Land back for the Christians).

While traveling through Spain, James couldn't resist joining the king of Castile in a fight in Granada. Bad move. He was soon dying from horrid wounds and rather perturbed that he couldn't carry out his master's wishes. Without further ado, he lobbed the king's ticker right into the heart of the battle crying, "Go first as thou wert want to go."

Luckily (if you're concerned about dead hearts), someone found the thing after the soldiers had gone home and brought it back to Scotland.

Sir Howel-y-Fwyall

In the 1300s, a young Welsh soldier named Howel did so well swinging his poleax while fighting with the Black Prince at Poitiers, France, that the prince made him a knight. The prince awarded him a generous, but horribly termed, "mess of meat" served to him every night (good thing he wasn't a vegetarian). When Howel died, the mess was given to the poor instead.

Thomas Holland

If you're going to capture someone, make sure they've got money. Thomas Holland, a young impoverished knight, captured and ransomed the ludicrously wealthy Count Eu at the storming of Caen, France, in 1346. This move made him a very rich man. To make it the perfect storybook ending, he married a princess called Joan the Fair Maid of Kent (said to have been the most beautiful woman of the age) and became an earl. Don't some people make you sick? If it's any consolation, he didn't, apparently, live happily ever after.

Sir John Chandos

Probably the most celebrated knight on the battle circuits of the Middle Ages, Sir John became a Knight of the Garter three years after the Battle of Crécy (1346). In 1356 he also fought beside the Black Prince at Poitiers. Despite his wonderful record of bravery on the battlefield, John was more famous for the way he died.

In 1370, while just about to commence a battle, he strode toward the enemy line. Sir John had a habit of wearing a huge cloak bearing his coat of arms. As he approached, sword in hand, a gust of wind blew the cloak around his legs. John began to trip forward, breaking into a short run to correct himself. One of his foes, a squire called James St. Martin, who was to his right, shoved out his lance on the off-chance. Normally Sir John would have easily ducked out of the way but, as luck would have it, he'd lost his right eye in a hunting accident five years earlier and saw nothing. Added to  that, he hadn't had time to pull his visor down. As it happened, the lance went in exactly where his right eye should have been, so he'd have lost it again anyway (if he hadn't died the following day).

John, the Sixth Earl of Ormonde

An Irish nobleman of whom Edward IV said, "if good breeding and liberal qualities were lost in the world, they might all be found in the Earl of Ormonde."

In 1449 the bailiff of Évreux (a small town in northwestern France) was sent with a bunch of soldiers to Vernon (another small town in northwestern France). As ordered, the bailiff demanded the good people of Vernon to give themselves up to the king of France and to send him the keys of the town. John Ormonde, who was governing the town for the English, thought he'd have some fun and sent every key he could lay his hands on. The bailiff didn't find the joke funny and soon the town was under attack. Ormonde got an arrow right through both cheeks. The two sides decided to talk, which must have been difficult for poor John. Eventually, the 250 English were allowed to leave with their suitcases, provided the French agreed to tell the king that the surrender had nothing to do with them.

BAD KNIGHTS

Most of us like to think of knights as fine, noble gentlemen fighting for their king and country. This was only sometimes true. Many knights, I'm afraid, were cruel, dishonest, self-seeking ba ... ba ... *barbarians.*

In fact, long before the First Crusade, the Byzantine emperor Alexius I expected the Christian knights to arrive in Constantinople. Although on their way to help, the emperor remained very wary of the approaching knights. He regarded them as fickle and savage men who picked fights when a discussion would have worked. Alexius only had to hear the reports of how these knights behaved in their own backyards (when not out robbing and pillaging their neighbors) to realize how uncivilized most of them were.

Rightly so, the Byzantine emperor saw English life like the jungle. Both predators and victims hung out in their various castle lairs, eating and drinking in excess, while figuring out who to vanquish or oppress and who'd try to do it to them next. These knights terrorized the common folk, embarrassed the church, and posed a continual threat to the king.

The noble rank of knight had more or less devoted itself to warfare. While the knights' peasants toiled in the fields, the knights simply hung around their castles in jaded luxury. They yearned for the chance to polish their weapons, saddle up their warhorses, pull their squires out of bed, don their armor, say farewell to the wife, gather their soldiers, and hit the road looking for action.

For your average knight, the perfect day out included breaching a neighboring castle's walls, hearing the clash of steel on steel, and listening to the screams for help from the

wounded. He might also enjoy witnessing riderless horses idly munching the bloodsoaked grass and surveying fields scattered with dead soldiers, whose bodies were peppered with arrows and pinned to the ground by broken lances. As far as the knight was concerned, this all glorified war as man's highest achievement. The boring stuff like growing things, building things, making people better, or praying for their souls was not for the feudal knight. Knights embraced war and fighting with a passion.

Best of all, the more a knight behaved like this in Merrie Medieval England, the more honor and praise he saw heaped on him. The medieval knight became akin to a mini-dictator, king of his own domain, ungovernable, and not answerable to anyone.

An Englishman's Home
The very worst period of all came in the mid-1100s, after the arrival to the throne of the mild-mannered King

Stephen. The knights and barons, seeing the king's weakness, took advantage. Any form of law and order was completely forgotten. Hundreds of illegal castles were planned. The wicked men scoured the countryside capturing peasants and forcing them to build the castles. When finished, they became the master's servants, forced into virtual slavery. Peasants thought to have any money were thrown into squalid dungeons and tortured until they gave it up. The masters hung up some by their thumbs and smoked them like fish. Some peasants had burning things tied to their feet, while others had ropes twisted around their heads till their skulls split and their brains exploded. Many were thrown into dungeons full of poisonous snakes, while other peasants were crushed into small chests that were then filled with sharp, heavy stones till all their arms and legs broke. Or they suffered the popular spiked steel collars that made it impossible for the poor wearer to lie down or sleep.

These cruel knights squeezed protection money from the impoverished villagers. When their villagers' meager savings ran out, the knights burned the villages to the ground. Throughout the land, the feudal knight became simply a force for evil. So, when the idea of a holy war came up, there was always a lot of people trying to escape their lords, the famine, constant civil wars, and an agonizing new fever called Saint Anthony's Fire.

Geoffrey de Mandeville

Right at the top of the noxious knight league was a guy called Geoffrey de Mandeville. He ran down his estate in eastern England so much that for thirty miles around his castle neither an ox nor a plow could be found. The price of grain soared to 200 pennies a bushel. Poor folk of his fief died in droves from starvation. The corpses laid in the fields, pecked by the crows and torn apart by the beasts (hedgehogs, bunnies, etc.). Those that survived were tortured mercilessly for their money whether they had it or not.

By the Way

Geoff de Mandeville got his comeuppance. He was trampled to death at a tournament. Ha-ha!

Simon de Montfort

We're not talking about the English one—otherwise known as the earl of Leicester. This French Simon de Montfort was a Norman knight who led a Crusade on behalf of his countrymen. He ordered that whenever a castle was taken by force, everyone inside was to be massacred—no questions asked. For years he waged war against the powerful anti-Catholic religious sect the Cathars. At Minerve he took 140 black-robed Cathar priests and flung them onto a bonfire. At Lavaur 400 priests also burned, and their defenders were hanged. The famous lady-priest Giraude de Laurac was flung down a well and rocks were thrown down on top of her in case she got too comfortable. De Montfort was finally killed by a huge stone thrown from the

battlements of Toulouse by one of the women defending it—
"the stone flew to its proper mark, and smote Count Simon
on his steel helm so that his eyeballs, brains, teeth, and skull
all flew into pieces." Served him right too, says I.

Bohemond of Taranto

A famous Norman crusader who was strictly in it for the
money, Bohemond I was a tall, hugely built, spectacularly
handsome man with oodles of charm. But he was moody
and very resentful of people who were better off than him
(which was just about everyone). While chasing the Turkish
Muslims through Syria, his army of knights began to despair
their lack of food and had to sell their armor and weapons
to survive. To cheer his knights up, Bohemond roasted their
donkeys and then the Muslim captives (but I don't know
whether they ate them, too). Bohemond became one of
those generals in charge of the siege of Nicaea. It was
probably his idea to catapult the heads of his Muslim
captives over the wall. Nice guy!

Baldwin de Bouillon

Baldwin I went on the Crusades with his brothers Godfrey
and Eustace. Unlike his blond, handsome, and charming
brothers, Baldwin was dark, cold, and mean looking. He was
supposed to have gone into the church, but Baldwin wanted
luxury and women. When he left for the Crusades, he took
his wife and kids with him and was determined to grab some
land and treasure—he didn't care a bit about God. The stories
of his cruelty are legendary. Once, while on the way to the
Holy Land, he managed to become master of the city of
Tarsus, by cheating his friend Tancred, who'd originally
captured it from the Muslims. He was supposed to hand Tarsus
over to the Byzantine emperor Alexius as part of the whole

crusader's deal but had no intention of doing so. When 300 Norman knights turned up to help defend the city, he wouldn't let them in, saying that they should continue marching. The poor tired Normans were forced to sleep outside the city walls. The Muslims (who hadn't really gone away) massacred them. A few weeks later, Baldwin decided he didn't want the city after all, so he simply deserted and left it to a bunch of pirates.

Despite his ruthless misdeeds, the horrible Baldwin eventually became king of Jerusalem in 1100, having set out on the Crusades as a penniless adventurer.

Richard the Lion-Hearted

You might be surprised to find Richard in this chapter. After all, wasn't he supposed to be one of the most dashing heroes England ever produced? True he was tall, immensely strong, blond, charming, and so handsome that friends and enemies alike fell under his spell. But that was the good side. The other was far more dubious. Richard had a foul temper, which came out whenever he didn't get his way.

His cruelty knew no bounds. In 1177 he crushed a French revolt at Barbeziex. He ended up with 2,500 prisoners and couldn't make up his mind exactly how to teach them a lesson. He eventually decided on three solutions. The first third he beheaded in front of all the others. The second third he had drowned in the river in front of the last third. He then blinded the remainder and left them staggering around with orders to proclaim the king's justice to whomever they met.

THE END OF THE KNIGHT

By the end of the thirteenth century, the whole knight business was in a pretty pathetic state. Most knights had blown their money on crusading or tournaments. Almost unbelievably, the actual rank of knighthood, that most noble symbol, went up for sale on the open market, like a pound of cheese or a leg of lamb. Nobody with half a grain of sense, however, wanted to be a knight anymore—it was too expensive. For a start, armor was becoming more and more complex, robust, and thick in order to keep out bolts from the newfangled crossbow. It doesn't take a degree in economics to realize that this change increased the price. Then there was the dear old warhorse. These big brutes (they often had to have several) cost almost twenty times as much as an ordinary horse, and to protect their master's investment they needed armor, too. Then there was the cost of equipping a small bunch of men to fight for the knight's overlord. All in all, the knight was having to spend nearly all of his cash on this—and he didn't like it. He much preferred to stay home and look after his estate. Who can blame him?

Compulsory Knights

It got so bad that, in the 1200s, Edward I ordered that anyone who had freehold lands bringing in more than the equivalent of about thirty dollars a year, had to become a knight—or else pay a large fine to cover the cost of hiring mercenaries. Many English gentlemen willingly paid this fine to not go broke. But alas, some knights became virtual beggars, forced to go to moneylenders or plead with rich townsfolk to survive.

So all that chivalry, like devotion to his faith and his lord and vowing to defend women, children, and the sick, went right out of the castle window as the boot became firmly placed on the other foot.

Instead of protecting their peasants, some knights preyed on them, made them work for no money, took whatever they owned, and gave them nothing in return. English knights had also lost what they found most precious—respect on the battlefields of Europe. All they were after was hard cash in the form of ransoms. A dead foe was no use to a broke knight, but a live one could be sold back to his lord or family for a castle full of money.

Soldiers for Hire

Often savage and unprincipled mercenaries had to be found to fight battles, if the knights refused to do it. These guys were simply hired killers who murdered and robbed for anyone who'd pay them enough loot.

Something had to be done, so Edward I eventually reintroduced conscription, which meant that every able-bodied man of a certain age was forced to fight for his country. Oddly enough, this actually worked well. By the time of the Hundred Years' War with France in the fourteenth and fifteenth centuries, Edward III had a huge army of well-trained soldiers fighting for their king and country once more. For the first time since the age of chivalry had begun, all men, rather than just a particular class, were willing to go to war for land and glory . . . and their king.

Knightfall

Meanwhile, with the introduction of new weapons, such as the longbow, the heavily armored knight had had his day. At the Battle of Crécy, in which the English longbowmen massacred the French crossbowmen, cruel English foot soldiers ran among the armored, unsaddled French knights lying winded and helpless in the mud. They rammed their long daggers deep into the eye slits of their helmets, killing them instantly. Who says the English were always gentlemen? (Actually, these guys turned out to be Welsh, but we won't go into that now.) All in all, 1,542 French knights and lords were slain while England only lost two. That's what I call a result.

By the Way

A well-fired arrow from an English longbow could pierce chain mail, a four-inch oak door, or bring a horse down from a range of 590 feet. One of William de Braose's knights was unlucky enough to be on the receiving end of an arrow that went straight through the skirts of his mail shirt, through his mail trousers, through his thigh, and through the wooden part of his saddle until it finally came to rest pinning him to his horse's rump.

Knights for All

Eventually, ordinary people, like rich townsfolk, could become knights. Unlike these days, when only the reigning king or queen can do it, anyone who was a knight could make anyone who wasn't a knight . . . a knight. The whole thing began to get out of hand, with the average knight making knights out of people he either liked or owed money to. He could even turn his little kids into knights before they even knew what the word meant—and they wouldn't have to make vows or serve any sort of apprenticeship. It was a complete free-for-all.

These days, as we all know, even aging rock stars, retired sports professionals, and failed politicians get made into knights or lords. So, I suppose we can safely say that the idea of the knight as a God-fearing symbol of nobility, ready to fight in foreign lands for the honor of his country and God, has really disappeared. What a shame!

KNIGHT SPEAK

apprentice: a person who trades his or her timed servitude for unpaid instruction in an occupation (kind of like an intern). You students can consider yourselves apprentices to general knowledge.

cavalry: the lucky, if you don't mind equine animals, part of an army that rides on horseback

chain mail: no, not superstitious letters, a kind of garment made of woven metal that protects the wearer. And if you don't wear one right now, a tree will land on your bike!

chivalry: the code of knighthood. And if you were paying attention on page fifteen, you'd know what I mean.

dub: most everyone knows what dub means—to give knighthood to—but I thought you'd be interested in knowing that this word dates to before the 1100s.

ecclesiastical: churchical (if it were a real word), meaning having to do with the church

feudalism: "the system of political organization prevailing in Europe from the 9th to about the 15th centuries having as its basis the relation of lord to vassal with all land held in fee and as chief characteristics homage, the service of tenants under arms and in court, wardship, and forfeiture" —*Meriam Webster's Collegiate Dictionary*. I couldn't have said it better myself, but I had to read it a few times before it made sense.

fief: the land a lord (or overlord) gives or loans a vassal on the condition that he supports the lord (usually physically, economically, militarily, wholly, etc.). Also called a fee.

Franks: a Germanic tribe who moved into the Roman Empire's European lands around the Rhine River in the third century A.D. Their empire expanded to include most of the land in the areas of France, the Netherlands, Belgium, Luxembourg, Germany, Austria, Switzerland, and Italy.

gentry: the upper or ruling class of people who bear a coat of arms (whether or not of noble rank), especially landholders

heresy: going against the teachings of the church, in this case the Catholic Church

infidel: someone who has no faith. To the Christians, everyone who is not; to the Muslims, everyone who is not. See how that works?

livery: worn by servants, a badge or clothing (like a logo or a uniform) that identifies their lord

lord: to those in the Middle Ages, a person with authority who has land due to feudal claim

medieval: of, associated with, or representative of the Middle Ages

mercenary: a soldier who works or fights for wages (not necessarily monetary wages)

Middle Ages: not your parents! Actually, this term refers to the time in Europe's history from A.D. 500 to 1500.

noble: a person from an aristocratic (genteel, well-bred, blue-blooded, etc.) family, whose rank was based on military service and the possession of land

page: more specific than apprentice, a young boy training to be a knight, while in the knight's personal service

peasant: of the lower social class, a laborer who worked the land (sometimes that land was even "theirs")

scutage: the payment a vassal or knight had to give to the king to get out of fighting. Money talked, but not for very long. Each new battle carried a new price tag for those choosing to bench it during battle.

serf: a peasant laborer who inherited his or her indenture to the land and spent life serving the lord of the manor

squire: the personal attendant of a knight. I could use one of these.

standard: an object (such as a banner) used to identify the leader or an important location in a battle. The standard-bearer is the poor guy who carts it around for his lord (hopefully he could fight one-handed).

sultan: another word for king. As the word is of Arabic descent, it usually refers to someone presiding over a Muslim territory.

vassal: a person who pledges loyalty to a lord and who receives the lord's protection and usually some land in return

FURTHER READING

Aldred, David H. *Castles and Cathedrals*. New York: Cambridge University Press, 1993.

Biel, Timothy L. *The Crusades*. San Diego, CA: Lucent Books, 1995.

Corrick, James A. *Life of a Medieval Knight*. San Diego, CA: Lucent Books, 2001.

Cushman, Karen. *Catherine, Called Birdy*. New York: Harper Trophy, 1995.

Gravett, Christopher. *Knight*. New York: DK Publishing, 2000.

Green, Roger Lancelyn. *King Arthur and His Knights of the Round Table*. New York: Puffin, 1995.

Hart, Avery. *Knights & Castles: 50 Hands-On Activities to Experience the Middle Ages*. Charlotte, VT: Williamson Publishing, 1998.

Howarth, Sarah. *Medieval People*. Brookfield, CT: Millbrook Press, 1991.

Leon, Vicki. *Outrageous Women of the Middle Ages*. New York: John Wiley & Sons, 1998.

MacAuley, David. *Castle*. Boston: Houghton Mifflin, 1977.

MacDonald, Fiona. *How Would You Survive the Middle Ages?* London: Franklin Watts, 1997.

Nicolle, David. *Medieval Knights*. New York: Viking Children's Books, 1997.

Pernoud, Régine. *A Day with a Noblewoman*. Minneapolis: Runestone Press, 1997.

Roberts, Jeremy. *King Arthur*. Minneapolis: Lerner Publications, 2001.

Tanaka, Shelley. *In the Time of Knights*. New York: Hyperion Press, 2000.

Temple, Frances. *The Ramsay Scallop*. New York: Harper Trophy, 1995.

Yue, Charlotte, and David Yue. *Armor*. Boston: Houghton Mifflin, 1994.

WEBSITES

Castles of the World
   <http://www.castles.org>
A History and Mythos of the Knights of Templar
   <http://www.templarhistory.com>
King Arthur and the Knights of the Round Table
   <http://www.kingarthursknights.com>
The Knighthood, Chivalry, & Tournaments Resource Library
   <http://www.chronique.com/>
Medieval Crusades
   <http://www.medievalcrusades.com/>
Medieval History
   <http://historymedren.about.com>
Medieval Life
   <http://www.medieval-life.net>
Medieval Online
   <http://www.medievalonline.com/>

INDEX

FitzThomas, John, 73–74
Fourth Crusade, 30
France, 10, 11, 15, 22, 24, 25, 31, 32, 37, 38, 46, 54, 66, 70, 75, 76, 83, 86, 87
Franks, 10, 11, 12, 29

Germany, 24, 25, 30, 41, 46
Gregory VII, Pope, 19, 20

helmets, 12, 42–43, 44, 46, 68, 87
Holland, Thomas, 75
Holy Land, 19–20, 31, 32, 36, 36, 74, 82
horses, 11, 12, 46, 50, 54, 71, 78, 85, 87
Howel-y-Fwyall, 75

Jerusalem, 19, 20, 22, 24, 28, 29, 30, 31, 33, 34, 36, 39, 83

knightly behavior, 25, 28–29, 34, 72, 74–84
knightly skills, 68, 69, 71
knights, behavior of, 18, 25, 28–29, 34, 72, 74–84; and their castles, 18, 54–67, 80; ceremony to become, 8–9, 14; cost of being, 12, 16, 85; definition of, 7, 8, 12; duties of, 12, 13, 14, 15, 35–36, 39, 86, 87; end of, 85–88; of England, 43,

45, 86, 87; equipment of, 12, 42–53, 71, 87; of France, 43, 87; of Germany, 10, 40–41; misuse of power by, 14, 18, 25, 27–29, 80, 81, 82, 83, 86; of Normandy, 58, 81, 82, 83; ransom of, 17, 69, 86; and religion, 18–20, 34–41, 82; training of, 8; types of, 34–41, 72–84; wealth of, 17, 23, 36, 39, 69, 85; weapons of, 50–53, 70, 75, 78, 82, 87
Knights Hospitalers, 34, 36, 38, 39–40
Knights Templars, 34–38, 39, 40

land grants, 8, 12, 16, 23
Longsword, Sir William, 72–73

Martel, Charles, 11, 12
Mediterranean Sea, 28, 31, 32, 39
Middle Ages, 10, 18, 20, 50, 67, 70, 75, 79
Middle East, 11, 21, 28, 39, 46, 59
Montfort, Simon de, 81–82
Muslims, 11, 12, 19, 20, 21, 22, 26, 28, 29, 30, 34, 35, 36, 39, 72, 73, 82, 83

ABOUT THE AUTHOR

John Farman has worked as a commercial illustrator and a cartoonist and has written more than thirty nonfiction books for children. He lives in London, England.

THE SHORT AND
BLOODY
HISTORY
OF
SPIES

CONTENTS

PSST! WANNA KNOW
ALL ABOUT SPIES?

Most people think of spies as dark, shadowy men with big brimmed hats, fake mustaches, and no friends. Most of the time they aren't (and weren't) anything like that. There have always been almost as many women as men in the spying game, and nine times out of ten you wouldn't have known if you met one. Just like zebras wear stripes so as not to stand out in the environment where they live, and chameleons change color for just about the same reason, spies are most notable for not being notable. Let's face it, your teacher, your dentist, that funny guy who works in the library, or even your own mom or dad could be one—and you would never know anything about it. Spooky or what?

So What and Who Is a Spy?

Spies are those guys who are paid to move quietly among a group of people to find out secret stuff that another group (the ones who pay them) want to hear about. Spies are thus sort of professional tattletales. So why would anyone want to pass on the secrets of those who appear to be their friends to people who appear not to be? Surely that's a really mean thing to do. Oddly enough, a spy can usually get away with anything—lying, cheating, stealing, even murdering, and still not be thought badly of—it's all part of the game called espionage.

Most of the time, spies spy for political reasons—because they don't like how another country runs its business. This was very much the case during what was called the Cold War between the Soviet Union's Communist government and the democratic government of the United States. This war started in 1945 as soon as the Allies beat the Germans in World War II. To be fair, these spies were almost the most forgivable ones, for at least they believed that what they were doing was for the good of humankind. Whether they were right or wrong is not for me to say. Either way, practically every country in the world spies on every other country in the world—it's a fact.

Example

Despite the Soviet Union's rather unexpected fall in 1991, resulting in the dismantling of the infamous KGB (its spy agency), Russia now boasts four intelligence services and keeps squillions of spies in embassies throughout the world. Other sorts of spies, of course, don't do it for nice, moral reasons, and they never care about high-flown ideologies like Communism or capitalism. They're the ones who work purely for the money. This sort of behavior is becoming more and more the case in big business, where huge amounts of money change hands for details about a rival's strategies or products. The recipe for Coca-Cola, for instance, is famous for being one of the most guarded and sought-after secrets ever, and rivals would pay a king's ransom for the hidden ingredient.

But . . .

. . . that's just the simple side of things. Have you ever heard of counterespionage or of such a thing as a double agent? This is where it all gets tricky. Counterspies or double agents are the ones that one side thinks are working for them but who really turn out to be working for the people whom they are supposed to be spying on—or sometimes even both . . . a classic double bluff. They often give their clients (the ones buying the secrets) a whole bunch of false information, simply to lead them away from the real plot. The best thing about this scenario is that the spy in question usually gets paid by both sides, a sort of double whammy. The worst thing about this

scenario is that when the people who first employed them, or even the second people who employed them, find out they've been double-crossed, they get very annoyed. That's generally how more than a few spies end up wearing stylish concrete boots and being shoved over tall bridges into deep water and seldom heard of again.

Mole Hunt!

Very often a spy will stay in the same job for years while leaking little tidbits of information every now and again to the enemy or business rivals. Not from the likes of hairdressers or gardeners, I must add, but companies where either the inside information is useful to another country (weapons etc.) or to a business competitor (car manufacturers etc.). These people are called "moles," presumably because they operate "underground" and for the most part invisibly.

Good Tools

As technology develops, so do the tools that a country or company can use to spy. Real life constantly leaves James Bond with his 007 pants down. There are pin-sized microphones that operate on their own (without wires), tiny little cameras that work in the dark, and computers that can hack into others even though there seems to be no connection. These gadgets are all commonplace. So much so, that really important meetings, political or otherwise, have to be held in unbuggable, hard-to-reach places.

Old News

But trying to find out other people's secrets is nothing new. Nosy individuals have been trying to get away with such behavior almost since the beginning of time. This little book will attempt to trace espionage from its very beginnings, tell you who were the best and worst people at it, and give you a little bit of the day-to-day life of a spy.

EARLY DAYS

Spying is one of the oldest professions. The problem with spying is that it tends to be done in secret, so a lot of the really successful spying operations went on without anyone managing to write much about them—good for the spies but bad for history. Obviously, this becomes problematic when writing a book about the subject, but there seem to be a few names that crop up every time I dive into the deep and dusty records.

Sun-tzu

Just like everything else, spying seems to have begun in China. Try as I might, I can't find any records of espionage that go back beyond 510 B.C., when a Chinese man called Sun-tzu, wrote a book called *Ping Fa* or, if your Chinese isn't up to par, *The Art of War.*

It was all about how to get yourself a real secret service with spies and stuff and how to use them when having a war—which seemed to occur all the time in ancient China. This book was so good that it became compulsory reading for Chinese generals and military men. In fact, the tactics of the World War II Japanese attack on Pearl Harbor in 1941 came straight from the pages of *Ping Fa*. When American scholars realized this, they decided it might be smart to get it translated into English as well.

One of the most famous lines in the book went something like: "Those who know the enemy as well as themselves will never suffer defeat." Also: "Foreknowledge enables sovereigns and commanders to strike and conquer and achieve things beyond the reach of ordinary men."

Pay attention to this next story because I'm going to test you on it later.

Sun-tzu came from Ch'i but lived in Wu. King Ho Lu read *Ping Fa* and made Sun-tzu head of his troops. Sun-tzu defeated Ch'u and entered the capital Ying before turning his attention to Ch'i and Ching. Clear? Good.

Sun-tzu described every type of spy and claimed that they must be honored above everybody else in the land. He liked the idea of seeking out enemy spies and being so nice to them (free takeout, etc.) that they'd come over to his side and spy on their old bosses while telling them lies about his troops.

Test
Without looking:
Who was Ho Lu?
Who read *Ping Fa?*
What was the capital of Ch'u?
Who came from Wu?
And, most of all . . . Wu cares?

Alexander the Great

The next person I turned up was Alexander the Great, of all people. Alexander, who lived in the fourth century B.C., was the son of the mighty Philip II of Macedon and had been taught everything he knew by the philosopher Aristotle. Alex loved the idea of passing secret messages and snooping on his own troops to see who was or wasn't plotting. His sneaky methods must have worked, because he used them to find out who had killed his dad. Later, these ideas helped when he decided to go a-conquering (as they all did). Starting out in 334 B.C., his armies managed to crush lots of different peoples—the Triballi, the Getae, the Illyrians, the Thebans, the Persians, the Lycians, the Pisidians, the Egyptians, the Tyrians, the Ouxians, the Mardi, the Scythians, the Massagetai, not to mention all the Indians (in India). And, after lunch, the . . .

A Clever Espionage Trick

Alexander was fond of sending identical scrolls wrapped around staffs. He hid the secret message within a fairly ordinary boring report. The parchment was wound around and around a staff in a spiral, and the message was written along it in line with the staff. Unwound it made no sense whatsoever. Wrapped around a staff of identical width it could be read again. Get it? This idea survived right into the twentieth century and became the blueprint for many codes. A thin strip of paper can be wrapped tightly around a pencil and the message written along the line of the pencil. When the paper's pulled out it reads as pure nonsense. Try it.

14

The Roman Republic

The Romans didn't create a massive empire without a large amount of undercover work. Many Roman authors of the time let it be known that espionage was widespread and that the Romans had a huge network of spies resident in foreign lands. They also had double agents (called *exploratores*) who posed as friends of Rome's enemies while all the time sending back lots of juicy stuff about their armies, like where they went and when. At home, they took the form of a sort of underground police (kind of like the Gestapo in World War II Germany), infiltrating any groups who looked as though they might be planning to attack their emperor or his men.

The *speculatores* were another bunch attached to each Roman legion as secret service operators. They even had a club called the *schola speculatorum,* where they'd meet and swap tall stories and tricky trade secrets.

Henry II

In the higher circles of espionage, a term exists and is used as a warning to all would-be renegades even to this day. It's called "the Henry II syndrome." It all started in the 1100s, with the serious rift between King Henry II of England and his archbishop of Canterbury, Thomas à Becket. The archbishop was becoming annoyingly fond of the doings of the Roman Catholics and the pope. Unfortunately, his old friend Henry most certainly wasn't. It was when the archbishop started excommunicating (throwing out of the church) lots of Henry's favorite servants that the king began to really get upset. One day Henry happened to say, almost in passing, to four of his most favored knights, "Who will rid me of this turbulent priest?" The knights, who were extremely anxious to please, took him at his word. That night they went to Canterbury (where the archbishops of Canterbury usually live) and promptly went at him with their freshly sharpened swords. Unfortunately, Henry hadn't meant that at all and suffered terrible guilt for causing the death of someone who had once been his best friend.

In modern spying circles, therefore, they use the term "Henry II syndrome" as a warning to anyone who takes a politician's or a military leader's idle comment seriously (perish the thought), or who simply carries out an action on their own to gain favor.

By the Way

It all turned out all right for Thomas in the end (apart from being murdered) as he was made a saint in 1173.

Blondel

King Richard the Lion-Hearted (the one Robin Hood made all the fuss about) was best friends with a French guy called Blondel de Nesle. Blondel accompanied Richard on his campaign in the Holy Land to thwart the mighty Saladin (head of the Muslim army). In 1192 Richard rushed through Austria on his way home to rein in his crafty brother John. But en route poor Richard was captured and held for ransom in a secret castle by the duke of Austria (they did a lot of that sort of thing in those days).

Back home, it seemed fairly natural and appropriate for the king's loyal followers to ask Blondel to go on a spying mission to find his boss—but he'd have to have a disguise. We next hear of Monsieur de Nesle in heavy disguise, dressed as a silly-looking traveling minstrel (bells on pointy hat and stuff), trudging his way through Germany and into Austria. Blondel paused outside every castle to sing Richard's favorite tune (favorite because Richard composed it). He also presumably had to pretend to be German. Blondel was singing away outside some old Austrian castle when he heard the faint voice of his old friend joining in with the chorus. The spying had paid off. Blondel dashed home to England, raised the

SOUNDS FAMILIAR

ransom that the greedy Austrian duke had demanded, and got his best friend, the king, out.

I'd like to report that they lived happily ever after, but a little later Richard died while trying to get back the part of France that he'd once owned. He was only forty-one. Rotten luck, really. He was hit by a bolt from the very weapon (the crossbow) that he'd introduced to France! *Quel dommage!!*

The Ninjas

Would you believe it? Those ludicrous half-men/half-turtles called the Ninja Turtles really existed (well, just the ninja part) way back in twelfth-century Japan. They were a subbranch of the famous samurai who were probably the bravest warriors that ever lived. Back in those days, big rifts existed between all the ruling families in Japan. But by 1189, a man called Yoritomo became supreme shogun—the Japanese name for a military leader. He was the first to train ninjas to go on special spying missions to find out what his enemies were up to. These very fit young men trained from the age of five. They learned to hang from branches for ages (for some little-remembered reason), swim underwater for long distances, walk tightropes (for spying on circuses), and make and operate machines to help them fly. Best of all, they learned *ninjitsu*—the ancient art of disguises and tricks to make themselves invisible.

CAN YOU SEE ME NOW?

Genghis Khan

The mighty Genghis Khan was born under the name Temüjin in 1167 by Lake Baikal, in Russia. His dad ruled the land between the Amur River and the Great Wall of China (built to keep him and all his Mongolkind out).

Temüjin took over when only thirteen and struggled to keep his position, as the rest of his tribe were always revolting (in every way possible). A legendary leader, a skilled horseman, and a fierce fighter, he soon had his tribe and the neighboring tribes under control. By 1206 these barbarians decided to make him their leader, calling him Genghis ("precious warrior" in Chinese) and Khan ("lord" in Turkish). Flushed with success, Genghis Khan began to look for new pastures to conquer, for the Mongols needed more grass on which to feed their millions of horses.

He began to wonder what exactly was over that Great Wall. So in 1213 he and his horrible hordes invaded China (and presumably ate all their grass). The rest is history and not for this little book, but it must be said that Genghis Khan became known as the greatest military leader the world has ever seen.

NICE GRASS!

His success not only lay in his merciless savagery but in his use of intelligence to figure out the weaknesses of his enemies. One of his best tricks was to send his most trusty scouts to his foes. The scouts claimed to be deserters and that they really didn't want to be Mongols anymore. When these spies found out all they needed to know, they snuck back to the Mongols and spilled the beans.

Also Genghis asked his traveling merchants and traders to double as spies in order to update him on what went on in foreign lands. A unique early mail service quickly relayed information to the lord and master despite massive distances. This involved a rider in a special kind of Mongol mailman's outfit, dashing at full speed (upon a horse, of course) between staging points that sat twelve fast-galloping hours apart and had fresh horses waiting. It was said that a single rider could achieve three hundred miles in a day (not to mention a very sore backside).

By the Way

This system apparently gave the idea, centuries later, to the men who set up the Pony Express in the Wild West.

Council of Ten (Fourteenth Century)

In Venice during the Renaissance period in the 1300s, the Doge (chief magistrate), Marino Faliero, headed a conspiracy designed to topple the sovereignty of the noblemen of the Venetian Republic. Faliero was found out and executed in 1355 for his trouble.

To counteract this sort of unsociable behavior, a group called the Consiglio degli Dieci (Council of Ten) was set up. This spooky bunch acted as official snoopers or spies. They controlled the secret police, were involved in espionage and counterespionage, and had almost unlimited power. They wore sinister masks at official gatherings so as not to be recognized but would open their long cloaks, if challenged, to flash the official insignia that was woven into their linings.

By the Way

Venetian counterintelligence agents successfully outwitted industrial spies from Genoa, another Italian city. The Venetians' sworn enemies were trying to steal their secret methods of making their internationally admired cannons.

Sir Francis Walsingham

If ever there was a time when England needed a real live secret service, it was in the 1500s during the reign of Queen Elizabeth I. Sir Francis Walsingham was her undersecretary and soon realized that far too many foreign, particularly French, characters hung around the dark alleys of London—probably up to no good. France, by the way, was England's very worst enemy and had a well-developed spy network. Walsingham got the Lord Mayor to keep a weekly list of all foreigners arriving and leaving the city and had routine checks to see what they were up to.

Walsingham became the ambassador to France in 1570, in an effort to cool things down between the two countries. Actually, if truth be told, it gave him a better chance to set up a network of spies in France. Poor Francis, by the way, had to finance all these shady characters out of his own pocket—as the meanie old queenie was infamous for keeping the royal pursestrings tightly knotted. "Knowledge is never too dear (costly)," Walsingham pleaded in vain.

He eventually came home in 1573 to become the queen's first secretary and a member of the Privy Council. Everyone knew that his real job was still to keep a watchful eye abroad using all the new contacts he'd made.

It was still costing him a fortune. Francis eventually went belly-up financially due to almost single-handedly financing England's intelligence service overseas. It was a shame really, for at the time all those fearful foreigners were spending far more on theirs.

This underfinancing was dangerous in other ways. When European diplomats realized how little the poor English diplomats were actually paid, they dangled bags of gold in front of them in order to gain their services. This

strategy worked on several occasions. Sir Edward Stafford, for one, went over as ambassador to France, but the Spaniards (who were planning to invade England) soon noticed how "broke" he was. He became their agent. Although found out eventually, he was never brought to trial. Dear old Eddie must have worked as a double agent, certainly giving the Spaniards trivial information but all the time keeping Walsingham up to date on them. Nice one!

Walsingham battled on, and by 1587 he convinced his colleagues (and the queen) that the biggest threat came from Spain (England's new worst enemy). He decided this because one of his top men (Richard Gibbes) kept warning him every five minutes of a massive armada (fleet) of 150 ships that had gathered in Spain and were, to put it mildly, all pointing toward England! As cover, Gibbes had posed as a supporter of the Catholic Mary Queen of Scots who the Spaniards wanted on England's throne.

Walsingham stepped up his secret service to such a point that he no longer just listened to what was going on in deepest Spain. Better than all that, he had people right in the thick of the Spanish court and even managed to influence the date for their long-awaited attack on England. By twisting the arms of King Philip's bankers in Genoa, he held up the loans Spain needed for putting the finishing touches on their fleet (guns, sails, flags, and things). The fleet sailed but was soundly defeated by the English.

There is no doubt that one of the reasons the Spanish lost was because England's little fleet knew all about them. Better still, thanks to Richard Gibbes, the English knew exactly at what time they'd turn up (2:15 on Tuesday). Thanks to espionage, England didn't become part of the Spanish empire.

Gilbert Gifford

Gifford was a young Catholic languishing in jail on a charge of fraud during the reign of Elizabeth I. When he was released, he went to work for Mary Queen of Scots (the one who Liz thought was trying to overthrow her) but offered himself to Walsingham as a spy in her camp. He read all her secret messages, which were left in barrels and wine bottles. Best of all, he was let in on the elusive code that the pope used for all his letters and stuff. This meant that Walsingham, and therefore Queen Elizabeth, could second guess just about every move the enemy made. Eventually, they were able to uncover the final plot against Liz, which led to the severe removal of cousin Mary's still pretty head on February 8, 1587.

Christopher Marlowe

Many people believe that the playwright Christopher Marlowe wrote quite a few of the plays that Will Shakespeare got the credit for. He was certainly around at the same time and was certainly very good at it (playwriting).

Marlowe was the second son of a Cambridge shoemaker and went to Cambridge University in 1579. He nearly didn't get his degree because, toward the end of his studies, he was hardly ever there (I know the feeling). Luckily, a letter turned up from the Privy Council in the nick of time saying that he'd been in London "on matters touching the benefit of his country."

Chris, as it turned out, was in Queen Elizabeth's secret service. Sir Francis Walsingham had been employing a few of the brighter Cambridge undergraduates (always good for recruitment spies) and sending them over to Rheims in France. Rheims was a hotbed for spies and counterspies. Pretending to be a Catholic, he got in with the duke of Guise, the king of Spain's friend, and had a great time finding out the names of Catholic conspirators stationed in England.

It all went downhill however, as that sort of thing so often did (and does). The next we hear of our Chris was in 1593, when he was arrested for reasons unknown. He was released on bail, but ten days later the playwright was dead, killed in a bar brawl. His killer, surprisingly, was given a free pardon, so it really isn't hard to figure out that poor Chris was probably intentionally murdered. Why? I bet Queen Elizabeth might have been able to tell you.

Oliver Cromwell

Have you ever wondered how Oliver Cromwell, head of the army on the side of the rebel Roundheads, managed to defeat King Charles I in the English civil war of 1640? Probably not. Well, I'll tell you anyway. It was largely because of his deep belief in the merits of spying. Despite the Royalists' best efforts to keep their mouths shut, the rebel Roundheads seemed to end up with secrets galore, almost solely through Cromwell's head of intelligence, a real master spy, the brilliant John Thurloe. Later, when in power, Thurloe controlled a network of listeners at doors, not only at home but throughout Europe, where there were hundreds of plots to overthrow Cromwell.

Thurloe, an ex-lawyer, became Home Secretary, Foreign Secretary, Secretary of State, Chief of Police, head of the Secret Service, War Secretary, Postmaster General and Councillor of States—all at the same time!—and with a huge budget purely for spying. Not bad! This meant total control, making his regime so tight that one of the Italian Council of Ten heard from the Venetian ambassador that, though England seemed completely up-to-date on what everyone else was doing, practically none of their own secrets ever escaped.

Thurloe did it by flashing wads of money at the Royalists abroad and at people in most of the foreign courts. "Good agents," he claimed, "cannot be gained but by money; for money they will do anything." Back in England, he divided the country into eleven districts, each policed by his own sort of militia. They intercepted practically every letter sent and offered cash rewards to anyone who'd snitch on their neighbors.

By the Way

The only reason Ollie Cromwell died peacefully in his bed was because Thurloe was totally aware of every single plot to kill him.

John Churchill

Back in the seventeenth century, John Churchill, a supporter of the Royalists and the first duke of Marlborough, loved espionage and spent a fortune on it. He was famous for saying in defense of its great cost, "No war can be conducted successfully without early and good intelligence, and such advices cannot be had but at very great expense." He was obviously remembering the Battle of Sedgemoor in 1685, a typical good-news and bad-news scenario. The good news was that a spy told the rebel duke of Monmouth everything he needed to know about the royal army nearby. The bad news was that he forgot to mention a very deep, water-filled ditch that just happened to run between the two camps. When Monmouth's army attacked in the middle of the night, the Royalist army awoke to the sound of men splashing and cursing and promptly rushed out and beat them. The even-worse news was that poor old Monmouth lost his head a few days later.

Czar Paul of Russia

Catherine the Great's son Paul I took his mother's idea of a secret service one step further. He encouraged everyone in Russia to snitch on everyone else and put a big yellow box outside his palace where anyone from a road-sweeper to a high-ranking politician could drop in secret information about anyone. It got out of hand and so petty that one poor officer got a one-way ticket to the freezing wastes of Siberia simply for wearing his cap at the wrong angle. Anyway, the whole idea backfired as Czar Paul, obviously thinking his yellow box would at least keep him aware of plots and stuff, was assassinated in 1801 by a gang of his very own army officers. Apparently this had been the result of a huge plot dreamed up by nobles and military men who were fed up with the czar's increasingly silly behavior (and presumably his even sillier yellow box).

Duke of Wellington

Sir Arthur Wellesley, the duke of Wellington, the guy who beat Napoleon in 1815 (Battle of Waterloo), was a spymaster supreme. Wellington commented, "All the business of war is to find out what you don't know by what you do." He sent spies to find out everything about where a battle was likely to take place, what the enemy commanders were like, and how their troops were trained. He wanted to know what they got to eat and probably how often they went to the bathroom. He would even ask foreign locals what they thought about the British.

NOT INVENTED YET.

Charles Geneviève Louis August André Timothée d'Eon de Beaumont

If it wasn't bad enough having a mouthful like that for a name, young d'Eon (as we'll call him for short) was brought up by his mother to wear girl's clothes until his early teens. Helped by his pretty face and slight build, d'Eon slipped in and out of women's clothes at will and seemed to enjoy it (no comment!). But, strange as it might seem, d'Eon was no sissy. In fact, as well as having a law degree, he was considered a superb athlete and the most brilliant swordsman in all of France.

He was soon noticed by King Louis XV, who had his own little spying outfit (called Le Secret du Roi), and was asked to go on a strange mission. Using his ability to drop into girl's gear at the drop of a chapeau, he was sent to the court of the Czarina Elizabeth in Saint Petersburg, Russia, disguised as a young lady called Mademoiselle Lia de la Belmont. Oddly enough, the czarina herself liked to dress as a man. Is this all getting a bit weird? D'Eon or, should we say, Mademoiselle Lia was asked to find out (and did) just how close the Russians and the British were to putting together a joint army. If possible, he/she was to get them to favor France instead (French diplomats had been banned from Saint Petersburg for years). So far so good.

It worked like a charm. The czarina thought the girl was great and made Lia her maid of honor. All the French court painters wanted to paint the fresh new beauty in town, not guessing she was really a man. Gradually d'Eon, while

continually sending coded messages back home, managed to change Elizabeth's mind about the French and even to stop any idea she might have of signing a deal with the British. So far, so even better.

Eventually, the czarina was informed of the girl's secret and luckily was tickled pink, thinking it all quite funny. She even offered our hero a high rank in the Russian army, which he/she gracefully declined.

It had all gone so well that the young man returned to France in a blaze of glory with a pile of gold and a miniature portrait of the czarina herself. The French king was also delighted and presented him with a jewel-encrusted snuffbox. D'Eon was then made a permanent fixture in the French secret service. Things couldn't be better.

One of d'Eon's most famous spying jobs was when he was asked to come to England (as secretary to the French ambassador). The French planned to invade England. D'Eon's real job was to find out the best route to take once they landed. But all was not well back home. The king's dreadful new mistress, the infamous Madame de Pompadour, had always resented Louis's secret service and attempted to weed out its members and destroy them. D'Eon sat on top of her list. The mean madame tried to get him to come back to France, even stopping his pay when he refused. Her men then tried everything—poisoning, kidnapping, having him locked up in an asylum—you name it, but it was all to no avail.

It was when the old king died that things really came apart, however. D'Eon was broke and needed to get home. He wrote to the new king, Louis XVI, and told him that he was really a woman and that if Louis was anything like his dad he'd get the joke and send for him. Unfortunately, the new Louis didn't—and insisted that he must never dress as a French officer again, because it was an insult to France. He could come home, he conceded, but he must always be seen as a woman. Hmmm, tricky.

D'Eon was forced to agree but had his fingers crossed when he promised to obey. A little later, he was arrested in France for impersonating a French officer (and a man). They shipped him back to London where, to qualify for an allowance, he again had to dress as a woman for life. D'Eon got the short end of the stick completely, but Londoners found it entertaining. There were massive bets placed on whether or not he was indeed a man or a woman.

The rest of the story is so sad that it almost doesn't bear repeating. D'Eon was forced to remain as a woman for the rest of his life until his death in a cheap boardinghouse in 1810. He was eighty-three and poverty stricken. His landlady, undressing the withered "old lady" for her final trip (six feet under), was horrified to discover the answer to the riddle that had kept Londoners guessing for years.

Sidney Reilly

"Reckless Reilly," as he was known, was the spy to end all spies—the man who could have outwitted and out-womanized James Bond with both hands tied behind his back. He even looked a little like the movie star Humphrey Bogart. Reilly was actually born in Odessa, Russia, in 1874, not Ireland (as he claimed). His real dad had been a Jewish doctor in Vienna, not a Russian army colonel. This made him not Sidney Reilly but Sigmund Georgievich Rosenblum. Being Jewish in anti-Semitic Russia, as you can imagine, wasn't much fun, so young Sidney, Sigmund, or whatever you want to call him, decided to run for it. Sly Sid soon became the best kind of adventurer, popping up all over the world, using the many languages he spoke fluently. One time in the early 1890s, he even became the cook on the British expeditionary party that went up the Brazilian Amazon—no small feat in those days. It was on this particular outing that its leader, the well-known spymaster, Major Fothergill, noticed Sidney's many qualities and offered him a job in the British secret service.

So, in 1896, our Sidney became a real secret agent (a double agent even) working in the Far East for the British and the Japanese both at the same time (really Reilly!!).

By the Way

Sidney Reilly took his name (Reilly) from a wealthy widow named Margaret Reilly Thomas whose husband, the Reverend Hugh Thomas, Sidney kindly helped murder at the end of the century.

Later, in 1906, he turned up apparently working for the Russian czar, earning an amazingly fancy apartment in Saint Petersburg full of priceless old artwork. But all the time, he remained a special agent for the British. Basically Reilly searched the world to find the most trouble and got into it, working for whomever would pay the most. He had no fear. At one time during World War I, he parachuted behind German enemy lines. He stayed, pretending to be a perfect little German, and gathered secret information at the infamous weapons factory Krupp Works. Reilly killed two guards when he had to leave rather quickly. For this daring mission, he received Britain's Military Cross for bravery.

After the war, Reilly became obsessed with overturning the new Communist Soviet regime that had taken over Russia. He traveled in and out of Russia with a pass saying he was a member of the Soviet secret police.

It all came to a bad end (or didn't) in 1925, when Reilly was shot (or wasn't) trying to cross the Finnish border into Russia. Neither the Soviets nor the Brits would say anything about it—more than likely because they didn't know. Some say he was executed in 1925. Others say they saw him walking about, large as life, in 1927. Whether he was shot or really died or is even alive now (aged 135) will probably never be known. All we can assume is that Sidney Reilly kicked the bucket in the same manner as he lived—shrouded in deceit, in double-crossing, and in mystery. Whether Reilly was really working for the British or the Russians is probably the biggest mystery of all.

One thing is for certain, Sidney Sigmund Georgievich Rosenblum Reilly was the most celebrated spy of all time. He alone laid the foundation for the spy ring that eventually wriggled right into the heart of British society.

The Boy Scouts

WHO ARE YOU
— WORKING FOR?

Did you know that Robert Smyth, Lord Baden-Powell, the man who founded the Boy Scouts in 1908, was once a spy? Better still, did you know that Heinrich Himmler, who headed the Gestapo (Germany's secret police) during World War II, actually believed that because of this affiliation the scouts had to be a branch of the British secret service? I wonder what he thought the Girl Scouts and the Brownies were up to?

Baden-Powell was a whiz with the old paintbrush and, while sketching butterflies, integrated outlines of enemy fortifications or weapons into the complicated wing patterns and sent them home. Another trick he used was to soak his clothes in strong booze and totter off toward secret military installations. Having employed a good snoop, they'd usually find him but, because they thought a complete drunk was no threat to anyone, the sentries would just kick him out.

UNLIKELY SPIES

Prime Suspect, Geoffrey Prime

Can you imagine anywhere more innocent sounding than Laburnum Cottage, Pittville, Crescent Lane, Cheltenham? This was the home of Mr. Geoffrey Prime, a highly respectable rep for a wine company, and his wife. Little did the neighbors know of the real Mr. Prime.

On April 27, 1982, a couple of police officers called at the Primes' front door and asked whether Mr. Prime owned a two-tone, brown and cream Ford Cortina (a crime in itself). They wanted to find out why it had been seen in the same location as a series of assaults on young girls over the last couple of years. Prime denied knowing anything about it. After the police had gone, Prime broke down and confessed to his wife that he had committed the assaults. The good lady said she would support him through all the trials and tribulations ahead. Imagine her surprise, however, when having gotten all of that off of his chest, her hubby threw caution to the wind and confessed to having been a Soviet spy for the last fourteen years. I suppose he must have thought that having confessed to being a pervert, a spy wouldn't seem so bad.

The next day Prime went to the police and told all. Well almost all—he somehow forgot to mention the spying part. The shocked Mrs. Prime, waiting patiently at home, still didn't believe her old man had been a spy until she peeked into his briefcase (still on the hall table) and found, under a false bottom, a full set of spying tools— right down to a miniature camera, invisible-writing equipment, and a bunch of special little codebooks. After asking the advice of her priest, lawyer, and doctor (why not the milkman, I ask), she decided to spill the beans to the cops. Even the officer in charge didn't believe that the rather dorky looking Prime could possibly have been

such a dark and mysterious figure. But when he saw the old miniature spy equipment, he immediately called the police department's Special Branch, which arrived before he'd even put the phone down.

On further investigation, they found that Prime wasn't just a little man sending the odd piece of not-very-important stuff to the Soviets, but a big-time main agent dealing in the sort of secrets that made their eyes water.

Why Had He Dunnit?

Prime had been an unhappy loner as a kid and had been assaulted by an adult when very young. When he did his compulsory military training at eighteen, he was found to be good at languages, if not much else. Prime chose Russian, and, although turning out to be not as good as they at first thought, he did end up snooping on Russian voice transmissions at a Royal Air Force base in West Berlin, Germany. He was then promoted to sergeant.

When arrested for spying, Prime said that he'd gone over to the Soviets of his own accord. But it later looked much more probable that the Russkies had somehow discovered his unhealthy interest in young girls and had blackmailed him. They wanted to know how much the Brits knew of their operations and which codes they had already cracked. Prime tattled so well—and it pleased the Soviets so much—that he was sent to a special spy school at KGB headquarters in East Berlin, East Germany, where he was given a complete spy kit and, of course, money. It was all terribly ironic. While Prime was being checked out for an incredibly important security job in Britain (which he passed with flying colors), he was actually learning how to spy on them. What a joke!

His new British job required Prime to continue to listen in on top-secret Russian technical conversations and report what they were saying to British Intelligence. What he actually did was tell the Russians which of their lines of communication he was tapping so that they could pass  lots of inaccurate hogwash to anyone listening. All this occurred in 1969, and Prime continued spying for years, despite being intensively examined six times by British Intelligence. He was so convincing that the British promoted him in 1975. He then found himself working among top-secret material that came over by satellite from the Central Intelligence Agency (CIA).

When eventually the KGB decided that Prime was of no further use, they cunningly decided to throw him to the wolves by wining and dining him in public with well-known Soviet agents at top Viennese restaurants. They hoped that the British agents known to use the same places would spot Prime and then handle the situation in the usual way. But although the Russkies flaunted him in all the fanciest hotels and restaurants, they weren't spotted once by the British agents. Prime worked for another two years before being arrested, as we now know, on a pure fluke.

The Special Branch originally considered him a sad, inadequate, perverted man. Shocked, they realized he was an incredibly clever and important Soviet agent who, during his time, removed, photographed, and passed on countless top-secret documents. Geoffrey Prime was sentenced to thirty-five years for spying and a further three for indecent assault on children.

Sir Anthony Blunt

Here is the headline news from November 20, 1979.

A shocked House of Commons heard today that the queen's distinguished art adviser and friend, Sir Anthony Blunt, 72, is a Russian spy. He was the notorious fourth man in the famous Burgess, Maclean, and Philby affair whom all the secret services had been trying to track down for years. Sir Anthony will, of course, be immediately stripped of his knighthood.

This was the final link in a story that had intrigued the world of espionage for years. It all began back in 1926 at Cambridge University, when the young, gawky, idealistic, but nonetheless brilliant, vicar's son (not to mention relative of the late Queen Mother) became a tutor as soon as he'd finished his studies. At that time, a lot of the fashionable Cambridge undergrads were carried away with the idea that Britain, the United States, and Western Europe were sliding farther into the hideous world of capitalism. These undergrads

wanted these countries to follow the bleak path of Communist Russia. Blunt was the first recruited by the Russians in 1933, and his first convert was Guy Burgess. This pair became part of the "Ring of Five," perhaps the most famous spy ring ever organized by the KGB. Their first job was to help the Russians stop the Nazis, who were making warlike noises in Germany. Blunt and Burgess recruited Donald Maclean, the lesser-known American, Michael Straight, and lastly Kim Philby. Blunt's main job was to spot anyone else among the undergrads who might want to do the same sort of thing (and cheat on their country at the same time).

It was totally bizarre that Blunt was accepted by MI5 (Britain's counterintelligence bureau) in 1939 at the beginning of World War II, especially when you consider that he had been a fully paid-up Communist in earlier life. But accepted he was, and he proceeded to wreck MI6's (Britain's secret service) counterespionage efforts abroad without anyone having any idea what he was up to. He also let his Soviet bosses know exactly who was sending secrets to Britain and gave them names and addresses of everyone who worked for MI5. When he became in charge of surveillance (spy watching), he was finally able to tell his Soviet bosses exactly who was watching whom, where and when, whichever side they were on. Anthony Blunt was actually the perfect spy.

All through this period, Blunt managed to keep his job as deputy director of the very cool Courtauld Institute of Art. He even met his spymates in his London office, using the office's equipment to copy important documents that he sent on to Russia. A lot of the stuff he sent—regarding the exact location of the soon-to-be-happening Normandy landings, for example—would have cost thousands of Allied lives had his Soviet bosses acted on it.

Blunt left MI5 after the war to be the incredibly important Surveyor of Pictures for King George VI. This provided excellent cover for his other new job as messenger boy for Soviet spies, at the same time giving them any information he could wheedle out of his old colleagues in MI5. Things eventually became hot for Blunt, when his old college friends Burgess and Maclean escaped to Russia. He refused to go himself, purely because working for Buckingham Palace was such an easy task. Despite being interrogated by the British intelligence services practically every five minutes, (they were sure he must be up to something), he continued to pass messages to and fro for years.

In 1963 the game was suddenly up, when a former Soviet spy working oddly enough as President John Kennedy's art adviser, suddenly confessed all and named Blunt as the agent who'd recruited him. Amazingly, Blunt was told that if he spilled the beans, naming names and explaining codes, they wouldn't prosecute him. Odd. Anyone else would have received execution for high treason. It's thought that his high-up royal connections saved him. For whatever reasons, it appears that Blunt did confess all.

Or did he? All the information he gave under oath appears to have been a bunch of lies designed to throw the British off the real track. Either way, his lurid career seemed to have been forgotten. Years later he was even knighted for work carried out for—get ready—MI5!

In 1983 a book came out telling the whole sorry story of Burgess, Maclean, and, much more to the point, Blunt. This time the game was up for good, and the country was after his traitorous hide. Blunt, at the age of seventy-six, died broken and alone in 1983, a disgrace to all who knew him.

Ian Fleming

You'd never think that the guy who created James Bond knew a lot about real espionage, would you? You'd be wrong. Not only did Ian Fleming know a lot about it, he'd been in it up to his suave and sophisticated neck for most of his working life—before deciding to write. Not only that, but our Ian was a lot like Mr. Bond himself.

Son of wealthy parents, a playboy around London, and bored with life as a stockbroker, young Ian craved excitement. He eventually met someone in the British naval intelligence, who was looking for bright young guys who were prepared to do just about anything as long as it was dangerous and the

money was good. Fleming was perfect—mad as a hatter, brave as a bulldog, and with ideas galore.

Fleming's first solo job, during World War II, was for Room 39 (his department's nickname) and involved Rudolf Hess (deputy leader of the Nazi Party). Fleming believed that if he could get one of the Nazis' top men to defect to Britain, it would strike fear into the Germans. He chose the infamous Hess purely because of his one weakness, he was deeply into astrology (star signs). Fleming managed to get in touch with the two Swiss astrologers often used by high-ranking German officers. Fleming told them to tell Hess that his big moment of truth was near—he'd been chosen by the fickle finger of fate to go to Britain and smoke big pipe of peace with Britain's prime minister, Winston Churchill. This, without any doubt, would make him the greatest and most popular man in the whole wide world. In 1941 Hess swallowed the bait big time. He borrowed a Messerschmitt fighter and flew it to Scotland, where he ordered the somewhat awestruck local police to take him to their leader.

Oh dear, instead of being delighted, the British government, including Mr. Churchill, saw him not only as an embarrassment but as potentially dangerous. They were worried that he might shine a torch on all the high-up Britons (including the king's brother, the duke of Windsor), who'd been having cozy fireside chats with the top German leader, Adolf Hitler. The government, therefore, let it be known that Hess was a total loony and no use to man nor beast. Hess went to jail and stayed there until he died in 1989.

By the Way

Hitler went crazy when the story got out and had every single clairvoyant, astrologer, or fortune-teller arrested. Their craft, art, or whatever you might call it, was banned in Germany.

YOU'RE GOING ON A LONG JOURNEY – TO JAIL.

James Bond—sorry—Ian Fleming (code name 17F) was a real life spy. He broke into safes in foreign consulates, photographed secret documents, made casts of keys, stole never-seen-before enemy aircraft engines, and even kidnapped the first German one-man submarine, complete with dead driver. After the war, he promised a friend that he'd write "the spy story to end all spy stories." And didn't he do well!

The Real James Bond

Everyone's heard of James Bond. In fact, some people would find it difficult to name another spy. But did anyone like him really exist? Legend has it that he was just a huge mishmash of all the agents Ian Fleming had ever met—with a great dollop of idealism thrown in. "M," on the other hand, was really a guy called Maxwell Knight, onetime boss of MI5 and a brilliant spy catcher. Fleming got the idea of the one letter name from a guy called Vernon Kell—code name "Major K."

The British secret services were born in 1909. Bond's forerunners consisted of a three-officer outfit. Their back-up team included a secretary, a cleaning lady, and a simple motto: "Trust no one." Since World War I, the number of agents rose to ten. But however amateur the British had been, the German agents were even worse. Practically all their devices and tricks were known by the British.

The dashing, one-man hit squad that was James Bond did not exist, nor did anyone remotely like him. Apart from anything else, if his hazardous lifestyle hadn't killed him, his self-indulgence would have. It's been calculated that he'd have slept with over seventy women a year, smoked seventy unfiltered black Russian cigarettes a day, and drunk enough martinis (shaken not stirred) to kill a bar full of people. He was licensed to kill all right—himself!!

The Krogers

As a kid, I sometimes rode my bike down Cranley Drive in the boring London suburb of Ruislip near my childhood home. I must have passed number 45 when the Krogers lived there. So what? I hear you cry. The Krogers turned out to be a couple of the most famous Soviet spies ever to live in Britain. And 45 Cranley Drive became the headquarters of one of the most infamous Communist spy rings run by one of Russia's cleverest agents. But why Ruislip? Easy! Because nothing ever happens there! Brilliant! Back to the plot.

ME

Nobody noticed the well-dressed, good-looking man with the small briefcase who visited the dull-as-dishwater Krogers every few weeks for supper. He was Konon Molody (Gordon Lonsdale).

Gordon Lonsdale/Konon Molody

Comrade Molody was a famous Soviet war hero who could speak practically every language backward. He was asked to spy on Britain—a great honor. His controllers wanted to know all about British and American airbases. (By the way, did I forget to mention there was a huge American base at West Ruislip?)

In 1955, disguised as a Canadian businessman and carrying the passport of a certain missing Gordon Lonsdale, Konon Molody arrived in Britain. Lonsdale/Molody set up several lucrative businesses, including supplying stuff like jukeboxes and bubblegum machines to places like airbases (fancy that). He even invented a car burglar alarm that won him the coveted Gold Medal at the Brussels International Trade Fair for the best British entry. With all that and the money he received from the Soviets, he was soon spending cash like it was going out of style. This tended to make one rather popular in the 1950s (or any time, come to think of it). It didn't take long before the very best people began to appear at his ritzy, no-expense-spared parties. Under the cover of his businesses, the suave, handsome company director traveled the country, but his real purpose was to make friends with anyone who had anything to do with weapons or intelligence organizations.

It was in this way that Lonsdale met the Krogers, Russian agents who'd fled from the United States when they were about to be uncovered. In their house on Cranley Drive, they had a full set of spying equipment right down to a radio that could connect with anywhere in the world. Lonsdale used them to send all his snippets of information back home to the old country (i.e., the Soviet Union).

This all went along just fine until Lonsdale met Harry Houghton—then it went even finer. Okay, Houghton was a secretary, but it was where he was a secretary that was important. He worked at the top-secret Admiralty Underwater Weapons Establishment in southern England. The KGB had dug around and found out that the otherwise colorless clerk had been somewhat of a bad boy in early life—selling stuff on the black market during the war. This information, admittedly not high profile, was enough to make him highly corruptible or at least blackmailable.

Lonsdale, now calling himself Commander Alex Johnson from the U.S. Embassy, soon discovered that Houghton would do practically anything for money, especially for untraceable cash. Johnson tricked Houghton into believing that he was getting all the secret stuff for Britain's U.S. allies. Soon the most classified top-secret information about the British navy and docks was winging its way over the airwaves from Cranley Drive—not to America but to Moscow.

Eventually, Houghton's lifestyle gave him away. How could a man on secretary's income afford a new car and an expensive new house, not to mention the lifestyle to go with it? MI5 put him under surveillance and watched all the swapping-of-bags-in-public-places routines between Houghton and Lonsdale.

Lonsdale was on the hook, and he led his shadows to his bank, where he casually deposited a small brown case. It contained a miniature Russian camera, a magnifying glass (so he could see the camera?), and a bunch of assorted keys.

From then on, it was easy. Lonsdale soon showed the British agents the way to Ruislip, but, cleverly, they didn't swoop down immediately. They wanted the big catch. It came on January 7, 1961, three months later. Under full surveillance, Houghton and his girlfriend, Bunty Gee, arrived at a London train station, carrying a large shopping bag. There they met Lonsdale. As they swapped bags, detectives from

Special Branch nabbed them. The bag contained four top-secret files and over 300 photos of plans of Britain's ever-so-secret nuclear submarines.

Then it was back to Ruislip and the Krogers. They at first denied everything . . . until even the most simple search revealed an Aladdin's cave of spying equipment and best (or worst) of all, under the floorboards, a device for sending coded messages at a rate of 200 words a minute. They were caught red-handed, and so was Lonsdale, and so was Houghton, and so was Bunty Gee.

What Happened to Them All?

Lonsdale got twenty-five years in jail, but upon receiving the sentence laughed out loud. He knew that in no time he would be swapped for one of Britain's imprisoned agents in Russia—which he was. Houghton and Gee got fifteen years each, and the Krogers got twenty.

The Undercover Pope

Giovanni Montini was a very ambitious man. He entered the Catholic Church in 1920 and soon had his eye on the top job—pope. The super-keen young novice turned out to be an absolute whiz at organization. It was no surprise that, by 1937, he'd reached dizzying heights in the Vatican (the pope's headquarters) and was hobnobbing with the actual pope, Pius XII. The Vatican, by the way, was to have an important role during World War II, acting as a go-between for all the different countries involved.

Anyway, Montini soon had his fingers in absolutely everything and was nicknamed "the man who knows all and sees all." He did indeed know everyone from diplomats to businesspeople to politicians. This meant that, if anyone wanted to have words with the Vatican, they had to go through Giovanni—no kidding! By the time he'd made bishop, he'd become the only choice to set up the newfangled Vatican Information Service—a polite term for an undercover

intelligence agency. But when the war began, Montini refused to take sides and wouldn't give away any secrets to either side.

Enter James Jesus Angleton, head of counterespionage for the Italian government. This chain-smoking Yale graduate knocked on Montini's door asking about an undercover agent, codename VESSEL. The agent seemed to be getting amazing information out of the highly secretive Vatican and was passing it on to the Americans. Angleton wondered if all this stuff was true or some load of junk supplied by the Russians or the Japanese, in order to deceive the British? The Americans were sure it was okay, however, and had refused to question it.

Montini soon corrected Angleton, saying that the information was nonsense and had nothing to do with what was discussed at top Vatican meetings. But there still remained the questions of who was doing it, why he was doing it, and who he was working for.

It turned out that there was just one guy behind the whole silly business. VESSEL turned out to be Virgilio Scattolini, a journalist and ex-pornographer who, having seen the Catholic light, packed up his seedy profession and ended up writing for the Vatican's own newspaper. When the editor found out exactly what Scattolini had been up to before joining his paper, he fired him. This miffed Scattolini a great deal, so he simply continued selling his own made-up Vatican "secrets" from outside the Vatican walls. Well, that is until Angleton and Montini stopped him.

The two men were suddenly pitched into the spotlight. Together they used their skills to organize the surrender of all the Germans and Italians in northern Italy, saving thousands of lives and the country from total destruction.

As for Giovanni, he went on to become archbishop of Milan. In 1963 the undercover wheeler-dealer became Pope Paul VI. He died in 1978, but his promotion might not have even stopped there, as there is talk about making him a saint— which is about as far as you can get.

Les Brown—Who?

In July 1983, helicopters and ships spent a long weary night trying to locate a lonely SOS bleep. In France, radar operators managed to pin the signal down to the Firth of Clyde in Scotland. The Faslane nuclear submarine base did much better and finally homed in on—get ready—a humble house near Glasgow. Fisherman Les Brown, sound asleep in bed with his wife, had left a radio distress beacon on top of the wardrobe. The device was apparently faulty and still giving out a weak signal. The vastly expensive air and sea hunt ended with poor Les being woken up by a helicopter pilot and a police officer hammering on his front door.

No great harm done, you might think. Unfortunately, a Soviet spy satellite picked up the signal first. Its ability to isolate such a tiny object shocked the Soviet-watchers in the West. If they could detect that faint signal, what else could they see? Not that the West had anything to complain about, as it turned out. Only a few weeks later, a couple of Russian jets caused an international incident by shooting down a perfectly innocent Korean airliner that had strayed into Soviet air space. They would have gotten away with the disaster had the Americans not been watching Russia's every move on their own highly sophisticated surveillance satellites.

WOMEN SPIES

Although Russia's famous spymaster Richard Sorge said that ladies would always be "unfit for espionage work," spying has always been one of the few professions with equal opportunities for women. This is probably because they are generally regarded as more trustworthy than men (please debate?). Here are a few of the most famous.

Aphra Behn

Despite her rather exotic name, Aphra Behn was probably Britain's first female spy, dating back to the seventeenth century. She married a Dutch merchant and, because of that fact, gained specialized knowledge of Holland and the Dutch (who at that time were always threatening to invade Britain).

Unfortunately, in those days, women weren't taken very seriously, so when she sent back secret messages from Holland claiming that the Dutch had rebuilt their navy and were simply dying to try it out, the poor lady was ignored. They should have listened. In 1667 a bunch of Dutch fire ships sailed right up the Thames River and brazenly destroyed the British fleet.

Louise de Kéroualle

The beautiful Louise was sent by Louis XIV of France to find out what the British were really thinking during negotiations for the Treaty of Dover in 1670. There were two treaties being ironed out. One (which was top secret) had to do with Britain's Charles II agreeing to allow Britain to convert to Catholicism (for lots of money and 6,000 French troops). The other, more formal one was about Britain supporting the French against Holland (for which Charles would get even more money). The French king chose Louise de Kéroualle, not only because she was gorgeous but because he knew she

was the kind of woman Britain's king really liked. She therefore acted as bait for King Charles, who predictably swallowed the plot hook, line, and sinker. He not only took her to his bedroom but made her the duchess of Portsmouth. They even conceived one of his many children between horse races at Newbury. I bet you didn't know that!

Lydia Darragh

During the American Revolution (1775–1783), General George Washington had to use the sneakiest of tactics to fight the British, from whom the Americans were trying to break away. At that time, Britain

was the most powerful nation in the world. Among Washington's many stunts, he had his troops dress up as British soldiers, go behind the enemy lines, and attack them from the rear (ouch!). He also allowed false documents to get stolen by British spies and even had fake forts built simply to fool the enemy.

But Washington was known best of all for his gathering of enemy intelligence and was even given a special secret fund for that purpose alone. Top of the spy pile was a quiet middle-class lady named Lydia Darragh, probably the most unlikely spy ever.

Respectable Lydia Darragh lived with her respectable husband (Mr. Darragh) at 177 South Second Street in the respectable city of Philadelphia, Pennsylvania. Both were devout Quakers and hated wars but not, as it happened, the individual soldiers who fought in them.

When the British took over Philadelphia, the officers seized all of the best houses (including the Darraghs') for themselves. As Lydia's had the biggest parlor, the Brits chose it for their strategy meetings. This decision, as you might imagine, really upset the peace-loving couple. The officers had no reason to suspect the polite, butter-wouldn't-melt-in-her-mouth, sweet-faced lady in the gray dress who took their coats as they arrived. But dear Mrs. Darragh was not quite as innocent as she appeared.

For months she used her fourteen-year-old son John as a courier, passing snippets of intelligence to her eldest son Charles, a lieutenant in Washington's army. Most of the time, the information was pretty small stuff (important, but nothing to win or lose major battles). Then one night, the officers suggested that she and her family go to bed early. Something big was afoot, and now-nosy Lydia wanted to know about it.

Listening outside the door in her curlers and stockinged feet, Mrs. Darragh not only found out that the British were finally about to attack Washington's army. She also learned just how big their army was (5,999 men) and what equipment they had (thirteen cannons etc.). The British officers then, to her horror, actually announced the night of the attack (only two days away), which would, of course, make for a complete surprise—not to mention massacre.

In the morning, having boldly received a pass from the Brits to go over enemy lines (she said she needed to collect flour from the local mill), Lydia scuttled off to get this scary news off her chest. She eventually reached the American army and spilled the beans—big time—to the shocked officers. Needless to say, when the British marched on Washington's camp, the Americans were so ready for them that the Brits didn't even bother to take the attack any further and turned around and retreated.

Nobody ever suspected Lydia or her family. No hint was ever mentioned officially or in any war reports. American historians, however, hail Lydia Darragh as a true heroine, whose bravery contributed to the successful struggle for American independence from Britain.

Emma Edmonds

Some women got so caught up in causes that they chopped off their hair and enlisted in armies as men. One of these women was Sarah Emma Edmonds, who enlisted in the Second Michigan Infantry as Franklin Thompson in the Civil War (1861–1865).

The daughter of a grumpy Canadian potato farmer, Emma was born in 1839. She never went to school because she had to work in the fields (picking grumpy Canadian potatoes). When she was eighteen, her dad announced he'd chosen a husband for her. She promptly dressed from head to toe as a man and left. (I guess she didn't go for her dad's choice.) When next we hear of Emma, she'd set up a successful business as a traveling Bible sales"man." Emma's wanderings brought her back to visit her old hometown, where only the family dog (name unknown) recognized her. Glad to say, he didn't snitch.

SHHH!

HE SMELLS FAMILIAR

It was around this time that Miss Edmonds (still dressed as a man) rented a room in the house of a Methodist minister who also headed the local militia. He suggested to "Franklin Thompson" (the name Emma was using) that he join the battalion when the Civil War broke out in 1861. Franklin/Emma agreed.

After leaving the army, Emma wrote of her adventures in a book called *Nurse and Spy in the Union Army*. She'd tended the sick and carried messages to and fro on the battlefield. She's remembered, however, for the "spy" part of the title.

To do the spy part, she exchanged her uniform for the gear of an African slave who toiled on the plantations of the Confederate States (the South). She cropped her hair real close, and then, with a bottle of silver nitrate, stained her head, face, hands, and feet black. She was so convincing that she passed through the rebel lines without attracting a second glance. She joined up with a bunch of slaves who were delivering coffee and food to the troops. Even these slaves didn't smell a rat (or a woman).

Emma was then singled out and shoved into a work gang of black male slaves, who were ordered to build fortifications at a Confederate base. After her torturingly hard day's work, she strolled around the base, making notes and tucking them into the soles of her shoes. After many adventures, she escaped back to the Union army and was taken directly to General George McClellan's headquarters to tell him what she'd learned. Emma eventually returned to her home, changed into a woman again, and married a local man.

Later, in 1884, a middle-aged woman applied for an army pension. At first, they couldn't get it into their heads that she was the same Franklin Thompson, but eventually they believed her and awarded her a pension "for her sacrifices in the line of duty, her splendid record as a soldier, her unblemished character, and disabilities incurred in the service."

Mata Hari

Margaretha Geertruida Zelle was the daughter of a rich and reportedly bad-tempered Dutch hatter. She became the most famous, the most mysterious, and the sexiest lady spy in history. She began her career as Lady McLeod, a cross between a belly dancer and a common stripper. She'd taken her name from her husband, Captain Rudolph McLeod. She had separated from the mean drunk just before reaching Paris in 1905. There she told everyone that her name was Mata Hari ("eye of the morning") and that she was the product of an Indian holy man and a temple dancer who'd died at her birth. Miss Hari quickly became famous throughout the nightclubs of Paris because of her willingness to dance practically nude at the drop of a hat. She also befriended any man who paid her enough money. Her best claim to fame, however, came during World War I, when she toured Europe, seducing high-ranking officers on both sides, French or German, and then selling their pillow talk to their respective enemies.*

Actually, if truth be told, Mata Hari was never that beautiful, and the secrets weren't often of much value. I mean, who really wants to know what a German general wears to bed? But that really wasn't the point. When the French realized, in 1917, that she'd been working for both sides at once and that neither side trusted her further than they could throw her, they arrested and tried her for treason. Her foolish explanation of why one single German officer paid her a huge sum of money was the last straw. She told the court, apparently, that it was the going rate for the pleasure of her company. They replied by letting her know that the going rate for treason was the firing squad.

Leonora Heinz

Leonora Heinz was a rather plain, rather lonely German girl who lived by herself in a chic apartment in Bonn, Germany. On March 1, 1960, she opened her front door to a good-looking young man called Heinz Suetterlin. Handsome Heinz carried a bunch of roses and said he was answering a lonely hearts advertisement. Leonora told him that he'd made a mistake, for she'd never advertised. But—let's face it (she must've thought)—how many times had she had such an opportunity knock on her door—and a single opportunity as

The Germans even sent her to a how-to-be-a-spy school in Belgium.

well! She promptly asked him in for a cup of coffee. Bad move number one, Leonora!

Suetterlin had been trained to perfection in the art of seduction. He learned from Soviet spymasters who had built whole training camps full of fancy restaurants, bars, and cinemas to imitate the cities of the West. Here young Soviet studs (called ravens) and women (called swans) were schooled in Western ways and particularly in how to charm the pants off important targets.

But why poor Miss Heinz? Well, surprise, surprise, she just happened to work as a secretary in the West German government's foreign ministry. They targeted her purely and cynically because undercover agents had spotted just how desperate she seemed for a man. It was a well-known fact that most of those extremely well-off young women employed by the West Germans had just about everything they could desire—except men.

Smoothy Suetterlin made Leonora Heinz fall head-over-heels in love with him. The love-stricken girl had no choice when he threatened to leave her if she didn't bring home top-secret documents from work. She was putty in his hands. Most lunchtimes, she rushed home from work to cook the lazy Suetterlin his lunch (beans on toast), while he copied the stuff that she'd brought back in a special false-bottomed handbag (a present from Russia).

In six years, she supplied over 3,000 documents, some of them reeking of stupendous military importance. The couple sent them to the KGB before the ink was hardly dry. At one stage, the Soviets were even reading documents and messages before the German foreign minister got a chance.

The couple were eventually arrested. Poor Leonora realized the ghastly truth that her now-husband not only didn't love her but didn't even like her—and never had. She hung herself that very night in her cell.

DEADLY SPIES

When someone in the twilight world of espionage becomes a problem, it often becomes necessary to, how shall we say... dispense with his or her services... um, permanently. This could be either because they know too much, because their services are no longer required, or because they've been found working for the enemy. In the past, most intelligence organizations have employed real hitmen, whose job is to get rid of anyone they're asked to, as quickly and as silently as possible—no questions asked. The nickname for this operation in the spy world is a "wet affair."

Here are a few of the most famous incidents throughout history (the ones that are known about, that is).

Nikolai Khokhlov

Nikolai Khokhlov was a well-known Soviet spymaster who had sent lots of his people into non-Communist Europe to get rid of so-called enemies of the state. One day in 1954, he was "asked" to do the dirty deed himself. His target was Georgi Okolovich, a fervent anti-Communist who lived in Frankfurt, Germany. It was good timing, because Khokhlov had long been looking for a way to escape to the joys of hamburgers and Coca-Cola in the United States. He decided to spare his victim and used him to get in touch with American agents. To prove he was who he was, he showed the American agents some of his special gizmos, including his latest Soviet weapon, a gold cigarette case that doubled as a nifty electric pistol, shooting deadly dumdum bullets tastily coated in cyanide.

His former Soviet bosses were understandably annoyed and decided to teach him a lesson. In September 1957, Khokhlov collapsed while talking at a Frankfurt meeting. He was rushed to a hospital, but they couldn't find the antidote to the poison he'd obviously been given. By this time, dark brown blotches and black-and-blue swellings covered poor old Nikolai. Blood actually seeped through his skin. His hair then parted company with his head in great black tufts. Worse still, his bones began to decay, and his blood started turning to water—he really wasn't well at all. The doctors eventually figured out that he'd been poisoned with the drug thallium, which had been exposed to atomic radiation (definitely something you don't want on your cornflakes). Poor old Khokhlov miraculously survived but remained bald as an egg and covered in hideous scars.

Georgi Markov

Georgi Markov was a Communist playwright who'd defected to Britain from Bulgaria and persisted in writing stuff that really got to the Soviet chiefs back home. One day, while waiting for a London bus, he felt a sharp prick in his leg. He whipped around to see a man picking up an umbrella nearby. The man said he was sorry and jumped into a taxi, which sped away. Markov thought nothing of it and went home to his wife and supper. Later, while watching television, he began to feel a bit sick. After another four days, he was stone cold dead, but none of the hospital doctors could trace the cause. At the post-mortem, however, they found a tiny little platinum ball embedded in his leg. It had been drilled and filled with ricin, a drug twice as powerful as cobra venom and with no known antidote. Experts believe it had been fired from a special miniature surgical device hidden in the umbrella's tip.

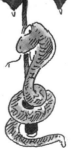

Buster Crabb

I remember this name because his disappearance in 1956 caused massive headlines throughout the Western world. Nikolai Bulganin and Nikita Khrushchev, the mighty Soviet leaders, had sailed to Britain to try, once and for all, to calm down the Cold War between the East and the West. They warned the British to keep away from their boat—the very latest in Soviet warships—which bristled with secret weapons and everything. Even Britain's new prime minister, Sir Anthony Eden, told MI5 and MI6 to keep away from the ship and the two Soviets. But naval intelligence simply didn't believe that was what he really wanted, and they couldn't bear having such a prize in their waters without being able to take a look around. They decided Eden would actually be delighted if they found out a lot of secret stuff about the Soviet boat.

The navy promptly set up radar on the cliffs of Dover so as to keep an eye on it and even made sure that Bulganin and Khrushchev's rooms in a high-end London hotel were fully bugged. Better still, they went for an idea first suggested by top war hero and experienced frogman Commander "Buster" Crabb. He suggested he dive under the ship's hull to have a good look around.

Heads You Lose

After the dive, poor Buster, a short, hairy, thickset man, was never seen again. Or was he? Some witnesses reported that they'd seen a group of Soviet frogmen wrestling with a lone frogman before dragging him onto their ship. A year later, however, a headless, handless body wearing the same type of frogman's outfit as Crabb's was found nearby and identified by Crabb's widow as her husband (I suppose she should have known—head, hands, or not). Case closed? Not quite.

As soon as the news hit the headlines, however, a Soviet sailor reported that the Russkies had nabbed Crabb and that he was safe and sound (complete with his limbs and head) in a Soviet jail. Then the Soviet government claimed that Crabb had actually gone over to their side of his own free will. They even produced a remarkably convincing photo of him dressed as a Soviet sailor.

The real story will probably never be known, but it's thought that Soviet spies had gotten wind of Crabb's plan to snoop around their precious warship and were down there waiting for him in a special little underwater compartment. They had probably dealt with him then and there in the way they knew best, so it looks like he lost his head after all. Either way, members of the British government ended up with oodles of egg on their, as it turned out, maybe innocent faces.

TOOLS OF THE TRADE

Let's imagine that you're a real spy. For all I know, you might be (the oddest people read my books). If you are, don't bother to read this chapter; you should know it all. The rest of you might like to know about the tools for successful spying, just in case. Here are a few of the absolute essentials.

Pigeons

Some people think that racing pigeons only live in sheds in people's backyards, but actually the clever birds have helped send secret messages, as far back as Roman times. Before World War I, however, using pigeons as a method of passing messages had kind of died out. But naval intelligence still used them extensively when the radio wouldn't work. The Brits even had a field intelligence division that used high-flying reconnaissance balloons to relay information quickly. Each carried a couple of pigeons. Right up to the end of World War II, in fact, Britain called on a "pigeon post" if no other method was available.

On July 30, 1942, the Royal Society for the Prevention of Cruelty to Animals gave a special award to Mercury for a special record-breaking flight. The daring bird flew 480 miles, without stopping for breakfast, lunch, or dinner. Across enemy lands and over the bleak North Sea, it carried an important message from a Danish resistance group on its leg. Over a hundred British birds had been parachuted in crates, but

WHY CAN'T THEY USE THE BLASTED PHONE?

only Mercury returned. I bet the rest defected and their descendants are probably living in complete luxury in Germany.

Invisible Ink

All spies have to pass messages between each other, and it's probably better that other people don't read them. Invisible ink provides one of the easiest methods, and there are many ways of making it. One of the best and simplest methods is to mix a little alum (aluminum sulphate) with water. You can then write using a pointed stick or an old-fashioned dip pen. When the ink dries, you can see nothing (apart from the paper, of course). Should you run a hot iron over it, however, the message will be revealed loud and clear. The trouble is that anyone opening an envelope to find a piece of paper with absolutely nothing on it might smell a rat. The answer is simple. Write a second message in pencil over the invisible one and tell your fellow conspirator to erase it before ironing the paper.

By the Way

If you think my method wouldn't work, listen to this. Whenever Germans were captured, the number of lemons they carried puzzled their captors. It was later discovered that they wrote messages in lemon juice over the normal ink ones.

By Another Way

The better-equipped German spies soaked their ties and socks with chemicals to be used later for invisible ink. When they got to their lodgings in Britain, they squeezed the items in distilled water, and presto, they were ready to write.

A World of Gadgets

Size is everything . . . the smaller the better in this case. Ian Fleming, for instance, favored a tiny cyanide gun disguised as a fountain pen. Others prefer dummy cigarette packs that kill (slightly faster than the usual contents) by firing poison darts. Also on your shopping list could be a watch that tells you exactly where you are in the world or shoes that have deadly retractable needles, etc. etc. The most important gadgets to any real spy are bugs—not the creepy-crawly kind, but tiny electronic listening devices planted somewhere in the enemy camp and designed to relay every word.

Bugs Abounding

Probably the biggest bugging operation ever cropped up in 1968 when the Americans and the Soviets agreed to build embassies in each other's countries. This was a nice friendly idea but potentially a little risky. The Russkies, suspicious as ever, employed one security expert to every two workers while building theirs in New York. The far more trusting Americans in Moscow just let the Soviets handle constructing it. Surprise, surprise, when they came to examine the finished building, they found lots of bugs—the place was riddled with 'em. The Soviets had mixed tiny microphones into the very concrete that built the walls—making them impossible to get rid of without pulling down the whole place. The Americans simply added three more floors to the top of the building at a cost of $40 million. Job done? Well, um . . . perhaps not. The architect they eventually chose turned out to be a Soviet spy. Whoops!

Codes and Ciphers

Secret codes go back many years. Religious writers sometimes hid what they were saying by reversing the alphabet (using the last letter of the alphabet instead of the first and so on). Greek generals went for the old parchment around the staff trick, while the Greek writer Polybius invented the 5 x 5 square pic, which is the basis of so many cryptographic (code) systems. Another method simply advanced each letter of the alphabet five places, a system used by Julius Caesar that is called the Caesar Shift.

Although it is believed that there is no such thing as an uncrackable code, the very best codes take so long to unravel that by the time they are, they are usually of no use. The Chinese have always relied heavily on memory for their secret messages, tending to keep actual coding to a minimum. This actually has more to do with their complicated writing system than anything else. Lately, however, they've taken to using the Roman alphabet.

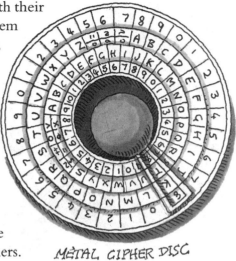

In Europe, the use of codes and ciphers in spy circles is as popular today as it was in the Middle Ages. Up until World War 1, the most popular codes were usually "substitution" ciphers. Briefly, cracking them involved

METAL CIPHER DISC
1802

comparing how often certain letters turned up in a hidden message compared to how often they'd turn up naturally in that particular language. Although somewhat difficult to figure out in those days, a fairly ordinary computer could sort them out in minutes. This is why Britain's decoding center at Government Communications Headquarters in Cheltenham has the most extensive computer system in Europe.

One of the great breakthroughs in coding cropped up in 1976. Adi Shamir, an Israeli mathematician, invented a way of writing to his friend Leonard Aldeman at the University of Southern California that only he could possibly understand. I won't attempt to explain it (on account of I can't understand it), but it involved the use of large prime numbers (those numbers that can only be divided by themselves and the number one). By a system of multiplication, a set of numbers could be achieved that could only be deciphered by someone who already knew certain secret prime numbers. Clear? It is thought that even the most clever computer in the world would take years to decipher the code. Even if it did succeed, it would only take a couple of hours for the cunning codesters to put the machine right back to where it started.

Enigma

During World War II, the Germans invented the Enigma Cryptograph. Despite looking like a cross between a shoe box and an old-fashioned cash register, this compact machine scrambled messages until they read like pure German gobbledygook. There were over 150 million, million, million different settings, and these were changed practically every day. The codes they spewed out became so complex that only a sister Enigma machine could understand what they were talking about. A brilliant team of British codebreakers worked day and night for ages to crack its funny talk, but to no avail. It was only when an actual Enigma machine was stolen and smuggled back to Britain (luckily with an instruction manual showing all the settings) that the British were able to figure out what the Germans were up to. This factor alone shortened the war by a good few years. When, however, the Nazis realized that the British were on to them, they changed all the settings (typical!). It took another huge team of top mathematicians and puzzlers a whole year to crack the pesky codes again.

By the Way

On April 2, 2000, a priceless Enigma machine was stolen from the museum at Bletchley Park, where the code-breaking team had worked. It seems rather ironic that a building that has been so involved with national security has only just begun to install its own security system.

By Another Way

After the war, in what looked like a kindly act, Britain and America sold off their old reconditioned Enigma machines to smaller countries at silly prices, urging them to use them for their most secret communications. How thoughtful? Not at all. All this meant was that the British and the Americans could decode all their most private communications for years to come. Does that make us clever or them stupid . . . or both?

No More Fibs

The lie detector—or, to give it its proper name, polygraph— has long been part of the paraphernalia used in the murky world of espionage. It's a tricky little gizmo involving four long, thin pens wired up to electronic sensors measuring pulse, breathing, and even sweating. One belt goes around the victim's waist, one around the wrist, and tiny electrodes are attached to the fingers to measure moisture (sweat to you). When switched on, the pens trace thin lines around a revolving disk of graph paper. The theory is that when someone tells a lie, the operator is supposed to be able to see erratic up-and-down movements on the paper. The British regarded the machine about as accurate as tossing a coin and really no more than an excitement detector. Not only that, but even if you could have detected a slight difference when someone was answering a delicate question (implying that they were fibbing), it was suspected by British Intelligence that the Soviets had a school that taught their agents methods of fooling the machine. This would become particularly useful if a spy wanted to pass on false information. As you will probably realize, the whole point of a lie detector would be missing.

By the Way

Despite changing its policy and dishing out lots of money on six brand-new, super-duper American lie detectors to test civil servants in crucial jobs, Britain threw them all away in 1985. Not only, I must add, because they didn't work but because the trade union wouldn't allow the bosses to use them on its members.

Satellites

No self-respecting spying nation should be without its own spy-in-the-sky Satellite Asset Management & Operations (SAMOs). The first ever was launched in California in 1961. It could, if it wanted, take photographs of a whole continent or of just your mom and dad lying on the beach. It can develop the pictures on board (without sending them out to be developed). It had a little satellite called a MIDAS, which, through its infrared detection kit, could tell if someone that it didn't like had launched a missile.

The Soviets, as we know, loved snooping and took to satellites like ducks to—er—espionage. They were said, in fact, to be far more interested in satellites for spying (with the eventual prize of domination of outer space) than putting a couple of guys on the boring old moon.

Nothing New under the Sun

Spying from the sky is not new, however. In the nineteenth century, European nations sent up hot air balloons to snoop on the enemy. During World War II, cameras were standard equipment on all fighter aircraft. These days everyone's up there. There are literally hundreds of satellites—Russian, Chinese, South African—all frantically taking pictures of each other and where they came from. The British are old hands at it. Despite the end of the Cold War, there's even a massive concrete bunker just north of London, where the navy keeps a constant watch on Russian ships, submarines, planes, or whatever.

Satellites linked to ships and extremely sensitive ground stations are now responsible for 85 percent of all surveillance. Huge computers work day and night to make sense of the jumble of signals they transmit. The British government's communication center employs a staggering 140,000 people and costs a large fortune to operate annually. Practically nothing escapes their notice.

By the Way

These days, cameras 200 miles above the earth can focus on stuff no larger than a foot long. The U.S. Big Bird satellites, probably the best in the world, can read a newspaper headline or tell whether a person's wearing glasses.

Did you know that in Russia the FSB (son of the KGB) is making all companies install a box (called STORM) so that everything they send through the Internet can be monitored?

Did you know that in the United States there have been various attempts by the government to stop ordinary people using codes on the net? If the feds get their way, they will soon only allow certain codes to exist—those to which they already have a key or those that are easy to decode.

In other words—BIG BROTHER WILL SOON BE WATCHING US ALL!

The Soviets Play Our Games

There is strong evidence to believe that throughout the 1980s, up to 20,000 Soviet agents snuck into the West with the oddest instructions. They were to buy any kids' computer games they could find and take them back to Moscow to be examined. The poor old Russkies had fallen so far behind with their computer technology that even the simplest computer toys yielded relevant programming information. For all we know, the same chip used to steer an electric toy dump truck could have been adapted to guide a lethal missile (scary or what!). The joke is, through examining all these toys and games, they practically caught up with the West—and, much to the distress of the CIA, it cost them virtually nothing.

WHAT NEXT?

If you think about it, the whole intelligence business since the end of the Cold War should be withering. The fifty years of fist-shaking between the Soviet Union and the United States is over. Ninety percent of all espionage in the last fifty years was all about the Americans trying to find out secret-type things about the Soviets, and vice versa, while, of course, both were trying their best to stop the other doing the same. It was all like a huge, hopelessly expensive, unnecessarily complex game of chess with neither side revealing its moves.

You'd think that with the collapse of the Communist bloc that the need for the massive Soviet intelligence system would be greatly reduced. This was true to a point. But despite the massive cutbacks after the Cold War, in military and intelligence staffing, both Russia and the United States find it necessary to strengthen their intelligence services. It's a known fact that both sides are catching more spies than they ever did during World War II.

But all that's understood. More important are all the threats that seem almost more serious than anything the Russians or Americans could ever do to each other. Terrorism, drug trafficking, international financial crime, and industrial espionage are all alive and kicking and gaining strength wherever you look.

Whereas weapons always used to be difficult to get hold of, you or I, or even the archbishop of Canterbury, could go and buy just about anything from a pea shooter to a nuclear missile tomorrow through the Internet, providing we have enough in our piggy banks. We could even, if the money stretched far enough, have a private army fully ready in a matter of weeks—so watch it!

The cost of fighting the drug war in the United States topped $13 billion in 1994, and massive markets are opening up everywhere you look—especially in all of those ex-Communist countries that have had the door on fun nailed on so tight for so, so long.

As for terrorism—the rise of religious fanaticism that seems to be spreading its tentacles throughout the world is so scary I can hardly talk about it.

As for finding out what all these guys are up to, unlike the old days, it's all become more difficult. Terrorists don't just call each other up from their mom's phone anymore, and drug barons don't e-mail each other every five minutes, and no self-respecting arms dealers would go near a fax machine—oh no. They're all into the most sophisticated methods of communication (like pigeons), most times outwitting those who are trying to catch 'em.

REALLY BARRY! HOW LONG ARE YOU GOING TO BE ON THAT PHONE?

Who's Listening?

As we speak, an enormous battle is going on in cyberspace between all the intelligence services that are trying to control the Internet and all the civil liberty organizations that don't want them to. These days the way intelligence agencies work has been changing. All that tapping, bugging, mail rustling, and office-breaking-in is old news. The perfect spy works with ridiculously high-focused mikes, laser beams, and untraceable cell phones. Best (or worst) of all, use of this equipment often doesn't require a license.

But wait a minute, all this is in danger of going out of date, too. More and more communication goes via the Internet using e-mails and integrated service digital networks and it is notoriously unsafe. The trouble is, just as all the security services use the very latest in computer equipment, all the same stuff is available to you and me, too. Not only that, you can buy software to create some of the most sophisticated codes known to humankind—off the shelf. The cat is still stalking the mouse, but, day by day, the mouse is in danger of becoming bigger and cleverer than the cat.

End Piece

Before you all go and hide under the bed, let me assure you that the future isn't all doom and gloom—far from it. Believe it or not, it has suddenly dawned on our brilliant world leaders that the enemy of humankind might not actually be each other . . . but international crime. Instead of wasting all their not-very-hard-earned cash on trying to second-guess what their counterparts are up to, the great powers are beginning to pool their resources. Who knows, you might even get a situation where the heads of MI6, the KGB, and the CIA do lunch.

SPY SPEAK

Ag and Fish: stands for the British Ministry of Agriculture and Fisheries. What's it got to do with spies? In World War I, it was used as a cover address for intelligence staff. Throughout the 1950s, many resting spies had desk jobs at the ministry, and it was understood that when a spy was said to be at Ag and Fish it meant he had "gone to ground."

agent provocateur: an agent sent into another country to provoke (stir up) trouble

biographic leverage: good old-fashioned blackmail

black bag jobs: part of an agent's everyday work—everything from burglary to bribery to kidnapping to even murder

bleep box: a method of telephone tapping, by which codes and frequencies enable the operative to break into various telephone networks. Used by most intelligence services.

blown: the term used when an agent is found out

bugging: listening in when you shouldn't

burnt: an agent who has been discovered and whose services are—how shall I say?—no longer needed (so he's retired, fired, or killed)

cacklebladder: making an alive person look dead (chicken blood, etc.), which often helps in blackmailing and forcing a confession from enemy agents

cannon: the guy whose job it is to steal back the money given to an enemy agent for information. Not a career for the faint-hearted.

the Center: nickname for the KGB headquarters in Moscow

CIA: the U.S. Central Intelligence Agency, nicknamed "the Company." The CIA is involved in both intelligence and counterintelligence.

cobbler: the guy you go to for a forged passport

defector: someone who runs away from either their cause or their country

demote maximally: to kill someone

dirty tricks: term used for the darker antics of the CIA

disinformation: anything designed to discredit or fool your enemy: false documents, false messages, smear tactics—you name it

doctor: the police. Hence, when arrested, they say "he's gone to the doctor."

FBI: Federal Bureau of Investigation—part of the United States Department of Justice. Among other responsibilities, the FBI protects the United States from foreign espionage and terrorist activities.

field: the particular turf on which a particular spy works

the Firm: nickname for the British secret service

fix: CIA term meaning to blackmail or con

fluttered: to be quizzed by a lie detector

footwarmer: an amplifier used in radio transmission

fumigating: checking a building for bugs (electronic ones)

going private: leaving the secret service

harmonica bug: tiny microphone that goes in a telephone

hospital: prison—how appropriate!

illegal: a top-notch Russian spy sent with false passports to foreign countries

in the game: in the intelligence industry

KGB: Komitet Gosudarstvennoy Bezopasnosti (yay, abbreviations), meaning the Soviet Committee for State Security

legend: a fake life story used by a spy as cover

lion-tamer: the man used to "calm down" a sacked agent who starts making threats. Not usually a very nice guy.

magpie board: a small bunch of keys, wires, knives, small tools, even a miniature transmitter, carried by an agent to aid in escape if captured

measles: a murder done so well that it looks as if the deceased died of natural causes

MI5: Britain's counterintelligence bureau, called the Security Service

MI6: Britain's secret intelligence service, London-based but operating mainly abroad

mole: an agent sent to work with the enemy or rival company in order to spill their secrets

mozhno girl: a pretty girl recruited by the KGB to seduce Western targets and report back to base on their secrets

music box: radio transmitter

musician: radio transmitter's operator

naked: operating alone without any help from the outside

nash: from a Russian word meaning to belong to one's own side

orchestra: long-term agents who remain dormant until being asked, blackmailed, or bullied into service

pavement artists: surveillance teams

peep: the guy who takes secret photographs, especially in rotten conditions

piano study: radio operation

Piscine: meaning "swimming pool" in French, the nickname for the French secret service (because it's next to a swimming pool—duh)

plumbing: the undercover work necessary to stage a major operation

radar button: a gizmo that pinpoints its carrier's position anywhere in the world, used to get him or her out of trouble

raven: a handsome guy used to seduce women in the line of duty (rough job but someone's got to do it)

safe house: somewhere secret where an agent can seek sanctuary if things get hot

sanction: approval for a killing

scalp-hunter: an expert who detects genuine defectors from fakes. They also rat on anyone who looks like they're about to run for it.

setting-up: trapping someone. Typical scenario—a pretty girl lures the prey into a room packed with microphones and cameras.

shoe: a false passport

sister: a member of the lower ranks of female spies

sleeper: an agent working in deep cover for years in a foreign country

soap: well-known truth drug

son et lumière: information on camera and microphone obtained in a setup (French, meaning "sound and light")

spoofing: snooping on secret establishments from the air, term circa World War II. Special high-flying planes with the latest in long-distance digital cameras are used.

spook: an agent or intelligence gatherer

sweetener: money or gifts used to persuade a "target"

thermal detector: a gadget that can tell where someone has been lying or sitting (measuring butt heat, presumably)

thirty-three: an emergency

turned agent: someone who changes sides

walk-in: someone who offers services or information without being asked

wet affair: an operation that uses a professional killer to eliminate a spy whose services are no longer needed

What's your twenty?: Where the heck are you?

XX Committee: double cross committee set up to control double or turned agents in World War II

zoo: police station

FURTHER READING

Cormier, Robert. *I Am the Cheese*. New York: Random House, 1994.

Fleming, Fergus. *Tales of Real Spies*. Tulsa, OK: EDC Publications, 1998.

Josephson, Judith Pinkerton. *Allan Pinkerton: The Original Private Eye*. Minneapolis: Lerner Publications Company, 1996.

Lyons, Mary E. *Dear Ellen Bee: A Civil War Scrapbook of Two Union Spies*. New York: Atheneum, 2000.

Mello, Tara Baukus. *The Central Intelligence Agency*. New York: Chelsea House Publications, 2000.

Melton, Keith H., William Colby, and Oleg Kalugin. *The Ultimate Spy Book*. New York: DK Publishing, 1996.

Rogers, James T. *The Secret War: Espionage in WWII*. New York: Facts on File, 1991.

Thomas, Paul. *Undercover Agents (Rebels With a Cause)*. Milwaukee, WI: Raintree/Steck Vaughn, 1998.

Wiese, Jim. *Spy Science: 40 Secret-Sleuthing, Code-Cracking, Spy-Catching, Activities for Kids*. New York: John Wiley & Sons, 1996.

Yancey, Diane. *Spies*. San Diego, CA: Lucent Books, 2001.

Yost, Graham. *Spies in the Sky*. New York: Facts On File, 1990.

WEBSITES

General Information

Cold War Espionage
   <http://www.cnn.com/SPECIALS/cold.war/
   experience/spies/>
International Spy Museum
   <http://www.spymuseum.org>
MI5, The Security Service
   <http://www.mi5.gov.uk/>
Secrets, Lies, and Atomic Spies
   <http://www.pbs.org/wgbh/nova/venona/>
Spy Fact of the Day
   <http://www.randomhouse.com/features/spybook/
   archive.html>
Spy Letters of the American Revolution
   <http://www.si.umich.edu/spies/>

Interactive

CIA's Homepage for Kids
   <http://www.cia.gov/cia/ciakids/index.html>
FBI Youth
   <http://www.fbi.gov/kids/6th12th/6th12th.htm>
The Spywatch Adventure
   <http://www.bbc.co.uk/education/lookandread/
   intro.htm>

INDEX

CONTENTS

PETRIFIED PARROT

WHO AND WHAT AND WHERE WERE PIRATES?

Does that seem a silly question? Almost everyone knows what pirates were—nasty, rough types with big hats, parrots, and wooden legs. They sailed in cool ships with lots of masts and cannons, yelling uncouth oaths and plundering and killing everyone who got in their way. Sure enough, all that stuff's more or less true, but it's really only half the story.

Almost as long as there've been boats, there've been pirates— Greek ones, Chinese ones, Viking ones, and Roman ones. Believe it or not, there are still a lot of mean modern pirates around today.

7

In fact, wherever there's a long and lonely trade route and an undefended prey, you'll find people trying to rob it. But the pirates I'm going to concentrate on—the ones you see in all the movies—are those from the mid-seventeenth to the mid-eighteenth centuries, the Golden Age of Piracy.

Before we start, I must tell you that there were several different types of pirates at the time. They went under different names, so I'd better explain, otherwise it might be confusing.

Privateers

Privateers were just as bad as other pirates, but they had a piece of paper called a commission (or license) from Britain's Admiralty Court. The commission more or less said that it was all right to do whatever they liked to an enemy ship (rob, murder, etc.) at times of war. The British government thought it had a good idea, because it was supposed to take the lion's

share of the booty. But many privateers—like the mighty Captain Henry Morgan—used their pirate's license freely, often attacking anything that moved, enemy or otherwise, and stashing most of their plunder before they got home. Many of the Caribbean islands gave out their own licenses to any old pirate who came along, purely for a share of the loot. The most famous

British privateers were the slave king Sir John Hawkins and, much earlier in the 1500s, Sir Francis Drake.

Corsairs

Corsair was the Italian name for privateer, but it later became the collective name for the infamous Barbary pirates who hailed from the coastal regions of North Africa—places like Algiers, Algeria; Tunis, Tunisia; and Tripoli, Libya. These scary seafarers, most of whom were Muslims (followers of Islam), terrorized the Mediterranean Sea in oar-powered warships.

Buccaneers

Buccaneers were British, French, or Dutch pirates, who hunted in and out of the Caribbean islands and later tried to get commissions to save their grimy necks when eventually brought to trial. Although ruthless and mean, they hardly ever attacked shipping from their own country. They got their name, by the way, from the first buccaneers who were hunters in the woods and valleys of Hispaniola (now Haiti and the Dominican Republic). These first buccaneers lived by cutting up pigs and cows into strips and smoking them. (Not like cigarettes, silly, but by hanging them up over a fire in a smokehouse—an ancient method of preserving meat.) The French word for this process was *boucaner,* and the boucaniers who did it were known for their disgusting smell and bedraggled, blood-stained appearance. Anyway, in the 1620s, all these boucaniers became fed up with

9

the smoked meat business and decided to move to the seaside, where they built a bunch of boats and formed a huge gang called the "Brethren of the Coast"—in other words buccaneers or pirates.

How Many?

Records seem to show that around 1720, right in the middle of the period I'm covering, there were between 1,800 and 2,400 American and British pirates prowling the seas, and roughly 13,000 naval seamen sworn to catch them. There are few records to tell us about all the others, but it's more than fair to say that traveling by sea carried enormous risk to life and limb in those not-really-so-far-off days.

Most pirates were recruited from captured merchant ships. Usually after all the fuss surrounding the plunder and pillage had died down, the pirate's quartermaster would step forward and ask if there were any merchant seamen who wanted to serve under the black flag (the skull and crossbones, or Jolly Roger, of which there were many versions).

JACK RACKHAM

THOMAS TEW

BLACKBEARD

BARTHOLEMEW ROBERTS

EDWARD ENGLAND

STEDE BONNET

Quite a few usually said yes, especially seeing what a good life the pirates seemed to be having compared to the drudgery they suffered (for almost no money). They threw caution to the wind and joined them. Most pirates, by the way, were aged between seventeen and fifty, with the majority being in their mid-twenties to early thirties.

Not All Laughs

But being a pirate wasn't all plain sailing, and it had more than its fair share of downsides. So be prepared for some hair-raising stories of dastardly piratical deeds guaranteed to make your blood run cold. So, heave-ho, me hearties, let's splice the main brace (whatever that means) and cast off.

ALL IN A DAY'S WORK

You may think that when pirates weren't robbing and murdering, they simply lazed around the decks, swigging rum, yo-ho-ho-ing, and generally having a great time. Well, you'd be right in some ways. Pirates had far less to do than merchant seamen, mostly because they usually had more than ten times the manpower.

Having said that, running a three-masted pirate boat of 300 tons or more, with enough rope to tie up, well, . . . lots of things, was no easy job, even if there were up to 200 of you. Old ships needed a lot of work to keep them sort of . . . shipshape.

Having said all that, pirates never really looked for hard work and preferred to indulge in their unpopular habit of stealing someone else's ship when theirs became a little, how shall we say, old and tired. Even so, a new ship would still have to be maintained if it was to compete on the high seas.

A ship, even in years gone by, was quite a complicated thing to manage. These days everything's made of metal, fiberglass, or plastic, so boats are relatively (and that's a huge relatively) maintenance free. But the old ships that sailed before people realized that metal could float were a complex web of wood, canvas, rope, and brass that required more than their fair share of looking after. Anyone who has had anything to do with wooden boats knows that you can't just build 'em, put 'em in the water, and sail 'em off into the sunset. No way.

Careening
Those old tubs needed tons of elbow grease. Sailors not only had to keep them upright, but they also had to keep the hull (the part of the boat in the water) as smooth as possible, so that they could sail at least as fast as the boats they were trying

to catch or the ones that were trying to catch them. This laborious process of cleaning and maintaining the hull was called careening, and the pirates hated it. What with all the barnacles and seaweed that clung to their bottoms (the boats' not the pirates') or the dreaded teredo worms, which chomped their way into the wooden planking, rendering it about as seaworthy as a sieve, the massive vessels would have to be dragged aground every couple of months.

The whole crew would then be expected to scrub, scrape, replace any rotten timbers, fill up the leaky gaps between the planks with oakum (rope smothered in tar), and then paint the whole thing with a mixture of tallow, oil, and brimstone before giving it a thick coat of wax or tar.

This was a filthy but necessary job that had to be carried out on remote beaches (pirates couldn't pull into ports like anyone else) and often in tropical weather hot enough to bake a turtle or rainy enough to drown one.

And Then . . .

See, I told you being a pirate wasn't all laughs. As if that wasn't enough, while they were ashore, the pirate crew would then be expected to gather wood and search for streams or springs to fill all the water barrels to the brim. Then they would be sent out with guns and clubs to hunt whatever walked, crawled, slithered, or flew out in front of them. Often this would be easy,  as most of the islands that they stopped on were so remote that the pirates' prey had never seen humans before. They'd let the pirates walk right up to them without batting an eye— and that usually went for the natives as well! Well, some of the natives. The smart ones knew what the boys were up to and chased them off their islands with bows and arrows and poisoned darts from blowpipes. Sometimes the pirates they caught ended up as a somewhat salty stew for the whole village.

Carpenter Ahoy!

Above decks, work had to be done to mend any of the structure that might've been damaged in the last few months at sea. Whenever pirates attacked another ship, especially if it was a naval vessel, one of the first things they looked for were craftsmen. Most valuable of all would be a ship's carpenter, usually an ex-shipwright, who would come into his own after a battle, patching up holes in the hull, mending broken spars,  and fashioning wooden legs as replacements for the injured real ones. (Sometimes the carpenter would have had to cut off the real limbs as well!)

Surgeon Ahoy!
Another great prize would be a surgeon. Britain's Royal Navy always had a surgeon aboard, and pirates were so jealous that they'd try and capture him if they got a chance. Pirates, you see, were always suffering terrible injuries, either in fights among themselves, or when attacking other ships, or just from all the terrible things that can happen when you get a bunch of men on a relatively small boat—like tripping over the ship's cat.

Cooper Ahoy!
Everything that was to be consumed on a pirate boat, be it bully beef, hardtack, water, beer or stronger liquor, was kept in barrels. Therefore, the next most important person on board was the cooper or barrel maker. He would not only make new barrels but repair the old ones and be an expert in how things should be preserved.

Very often craftsmen on naval or merchant ships weren't too worried about being captured. For a start, the pay was much better among the pirates. A carpenter on a normal ship, for instance, although being one of the highest paid members of the crew, would make less than two dollars a week, and the cooper would earn half that. The surgeon would also be among the higher paid and would generally be regarded by the captain as an equal. A cook, by the way, only received seventy-five cents a week on a nonpirate ship (and this was mostly reflected in the quality of food he prepared). Secondly, if ever a pirate ship was captured and the crew were sent to trial, these craftsmen usually got off without penalty because they'd been forced to join the boat. Obviously, they didn't talk too much about the share of the loot they'd no doubt received.

Slaves Ahoy!

Talking of natives (which we weren't), pirates soon grasped the idea that they could be captured and made to do most of the hard work aboard ship. This became so popular that the buccaneers even hunted down the slave ships that plied the seas between Africa and the British colonies in the West Indies and stole their cargoes. This happened so often that in 1724 a group of very annoyed merchants trading with Jamaica wrote to the Council of Trade and Plantations in London, England, complaining bitterly that the pirates were causing the "havoc and destruction of the ships employed in the negro trade on which the being of our Colonies chiefly depends."

Stealing People for Profit

The whole slave trade started when European explorers, particularly the power-crazy Portuguese, while trekking through Africa realized that there were thousands of natives standing around who didn't seem to be doing anything. The Portuguese had always been short of people to work their land, so these unscrupulous men rounded up the natives and sent them back home to Portugal or Brazil. By the sixteenth century, everyone, including America, was in on the act. Everyone except Britain, which cried, "Why can't we have a share of all this lucrative trade?" (Actually, British privateers had been supplying the American colonies for years, but that was unofficial.)

The British generally got what they wanted in those days (how things have changed), and by 1713 all the Spanish colonies were getting their slaves from the British South Sea Company, which made vast profits out of the Africans' misery. By the end of the seventeenth century, the main customers for slaves were the British owners of southern American plantations. The poor, innocent Africans were treated worse than dogs—branded, chained, beaten, and raped at every opportunity.

Bargain Slaves

To give you some idea of the value of slaves (if you'd wanted to buy one), it was reported that, in the early seventeenth century, a fairly average slave could change hands for as little as the value of a humble onion. Keep in mind that, for all I know, onions could have been very expensive, but you know what I'm saying.

Pirates' Slaves

One good thing came out of the democratic way that pirate ships were run. Some of the stronger and braver slaves were promoted and began to share in the profits. But it must also be said that generally pirates were as bad as anyone else when it came to ill-treating their black brothers. Often slaves who were on the run from the disgusting conditions of the West Indies plantations would beg to come aboard. But they would often be treated even worse by their new pirate bosses.

The End of Slavery

This disgusting trade in human misery ended first in Denmark in 1792. Britain followed in 1807. The U.S. Congress outlawed the slave trade, but not slavery, a year later. Brazil only finally gave up the slave trade in 1888.

Barbary Corsairs

If conditions were bad on normal pirate boats, you should have seen life in the galleys of the Barbary corsairs. The mostly Muslim pirates caused havoc on the southern coast of Britain in the 1620s. They came from the Barbary Coast seaports of Tunis, Tripoli, Salé, and Algiers and were mostly interested in slaves, particularly in the strong British ones. They'd been given authorization from their leaders to attack anything Christian, so for years they terrorized British beaches and seaside towns, dragging people from their homes and taverns to crew their boats. The corsairs would sometimes capture whole fishing fleets and merchant ships trying to leave the bigger southern ports of Falmouth and Plymouth. At one point, the authorities in Britain even had to smother the Lizard Lighthouse. This famous warning on the southern tip of Britain was turning out to be more use to the Barbary pirates than to British sailors. The corsairs figured that if they kept harassing Britain, in a few years the monarch would have no sailors left.

At the height of their success, the Barbary pirates had at least 20,000 Christians, mostly British, in captivity enduring terrible conditions. The long, narrow Barbary pirate galleys didn't have as many sails as other ships and relied on banks of oars (fifty plus) to propel them along at speeds of up to five miles an hour. This was especially useful when overhauling an enemy ship becalmed by lack of wind.

In the sweltering, stinking galleys, the rowers would be chained naked to their benches, expected to row for up to twenty hours at a time, and were beaten mercilessly if they so much as slowed down, let alone collapsed.* For food they would be given either a thin gruel or dry bread soaked in water or vinegar. When a galley slave died, as they eventually did, he'd be unceremoniously tossed over the side and a slightly fresher one brought in.

Many of the captives decided that they might live longer if they converted to Islam. On the good side, as Muslims, they got better conditions and more food but on the downside if captured, they'd be just as likely to be strung up as their new shipmates.

And strung up they were. In 1725 the Barbary pirates were driven from British waters by naval patrols that captured and hanged most of them with great glee.

* *They had to keep up with the strict drumbeat.*

ROTTEN FOOD
FOR ROTTEN MEN

Probably the very worst thing about being a pirate was the food. It was usually as bad as it can get and far worse than your grandmother's cooking or even the school cafeteria. The problem was always about keeping the food fresh. Instead of having fridges or freezers, pirates were forced to keep their supplies in damp, stinky, dusty, leaky holds, which made food rot as soon as they looked at it. If they wanted meat, they either had to salt it before they left port (salt meat's pretty disgusting anyway), smoke it, or, literally, walk it on board—baaing, oinking, clucking, mooing, and whatever noise goats make. Needless to say, the smell of the animals' quarters was only matched by that of the pirates', who, just like the animals, were not known to wash that often.

Pirates could, of course, catch fish but, as you might have guessed, they were a lazy, impatient bunch and usually couldn't be bothered. (Well, they couldn't be bothered till they absolutely had to be.) When a crew ran out of grub altogether, no creature—be it turtles (or their eggs), penguins, seals (apparently horrible), seagulls, rats, or bats—was completely safe.

RATATOUILLE

Eating ~~With~~ the Captain

It was not completely unknown for the starving crew to send someone down to the hold for one of the plumper slaves whom they'd stolen from some other ship or even captured themselves.

The motley crew of a ship that William Dampier, the British explorer, was sailing with, were the worst rabble imaginable. They once secretly agreed, at a time when they were running a little short in the grub department, that the only thing to do, if the situation got much worse, was to dine on the captain and Dampier—as they were the only two worth eating.

By the Way

Chicken eggs were called cackle-fruit, for obvious reasons.

If pirates hadn't made their living robbing and murdering, they could have called in at all the big ports, like other sailors, but because they were likely to get their necks well stretched if they even tiptoed on the beach, they had to stay away. The only fresh supplies, therefore, had to be stolen from other ships or fishing boats, plundered from small seaside villages, or simply hunted for when ashore.

Anyone for Lime Juice?

Because of their severe lack of vitamin C, due to their dreadful diet (no vegetables or fruit), pirates suffered from a horrid disease called scurvy. In the mid-1700s, it was discovered that citrus fruits, particularly limes, did a lot to prevent this disease and from then on pirates always carried as many as possible on board.

Hardtack

When everything else ran out, the poor old pirates resorted to hardtack, a sort of indigestible cracker made simply from flour and water. After a few weeks at sea, these crackers were usually

infested with big-headed weevil maggots that flourished in the damp, gloomy atmosphere. In fact, the starving men preferred to eat hardtack in the dark. Weevils should definitely be not seen and not heard.

Pirate Recipes

The crew of the seventeenth-century Welsh buccaneer, Sir Henry Morgan became so hungry on one of its longer voyages that the crew resorted to this rather gruesome recipe:
- Take one leather satchel (or anything leathery—shoes, saddles, harnesses, etc.).
- Tenderize by rubbing the large pieces between heavy stones.

- Scrape off the hair from the rough side with a sharp knife.
- Cut into very small bite-sized pieces and add anything you have left for flavoring.
- Add salt and pepper to taste.
- Roast or boil till soft.
- Serve hot to starving crew.

Salmagundi

When food was more plentiful, the pirates (especially the infamous pirate, Blackbeard) had a favorite dish that they always asked for in pirate restaurants. It was called salmagundi. Here's the recipe, should you ever have a buccaneer to breakfast, brunch, or supper:

- Take some or all of the following . . . turtle meat, fish, pork, chicken, corned beef, ham, duck, or pigeon.
- Chop into chunks and roast with cabbage (optional), anchovies, herring, mangoes, hard-boiled eggs, palm hearts, onions, olives, grapes, and anything pickled.
- Add lots of garlic, salt, pepper, and mustard seeds.
- Smother in oil and vinegar.
- Serve with as much rum or beer as your guest can get down his neck.

Indian Fast Food?

I'm not too sure whether this little incident should go in this section, but it is loosely to do with eating, so I'll go for it. Christopher Condent, a British sailor and latter-day pirate, was a quartermaster on a New York merchant sloop. An Indian seaman, fed up with being bullied by the rest of the crew, decided to blow up the ship for revenge. He was just about to light the pile of gunpowder he'd collected, when Condent—cutlass in one hand and pistol in the other—leaped down into the hold. The Indian, quick as a flash, grabbed another pistol and shot Condent, splintering his cutlass arm, but was himself hit in the middle of the head by the only shot that Condent managed to fire off.

The crew were understandably annoyed with the Indian seaman and, as the story goes, "hack'd him to Pieces, and the Gunner ripped up his Belly, tore out his Heart, boiled it and ate

HE'S TOUGHER THAN WE THOUGHT

it." What the poor soul's heart was doing in his belly we'll never know—or the recipe he used—but I'm pretty sure you won't find it in any books on Indian cooking.

And Drinks . . .

I bet you could have sold pirates any number of devices that supposedly converted seawater to fresh. Freshwater was a continual headache on pirate ships (or any ships come to that), because it was always stored in dirty old barrels and soon went putrid. Crews took with them as many barrels of beer, wine, brandy, and rum (grog★) as they could carry, and when they ran out of their own they would try their level best to steal it from the ships they overran. And that, dear reader, is one of the main reasons why pirates were nearly always drunk.

★ *Grog, by the way, was watered-down rum.*

24

Bumboo

Perhaps the favorite drink of all pirates was called bumboo, a mixture of rum and sugar, flavored with nutmeg.

Don't Try This at Home

On the downside, pirates sometimes had to resort to far less attractive drinks. On one occasion, pirate captain Bartholomew Roberts and his crew of 124 men found themselves short of water. They had only sixty-three gallons of water with which to cross the Atlantic Ocean. Due to poor winds, the days dragged into weeks and the weeks months, and the men, driven almost insane with thirst, were down to one mouthful of water a day. In the end, they resorted to drinking seawater or, even worse, their own urine. Many died, but the ones who survived best were those who stuck to their rations. There's a lesson in there somewhere. However thirsty you are, don't ever be tempted to drink your own . . . well, you know what I mean.

OPTIONAL EXTRA →

HANDY HOOK

ESSENTIAL CARTOON PIRATEWEAR

BIG HATS AND BAGGY TROUSERS

Most guys (and girls) think that the sort of stuff they see pirates wearing in the movies is great—big hats, baggy trousers, patches, etc., but the bold buccaneers weren't really as fashionable as they appeared clotheswise. Part of the job, you must realize, involved living in an atmosphere that was sometimes damp, sometimes windy, sometimes freezing, and sometimes blisteringly hot. Not only that but they were constantly being doused in saltwater. All of these things, plus the stray bullet hole or knife slash, have a tendency to make your clothes wear out quickly. Most times, however, they simply rotted off the bold buccaneers' backs.

GOSH-A BARE BUCCANEER

This, as you might imagine, was a huge headache for your average pirate, because he usually only possessed the clothes he stood up in. Therefore, next to a good supply of grog and a worthwhile haul of trinkets every now and then, clothes, which were very expensive before the nineteenth century (mass manufacture and all that), became extremely precious.

What Shall I Wear Today?

Not a common question below decks. All seamen from the 1500s who *weren't* in the British navy wore the same sort of outfit—baggy canvas trousers, called slops, cut off halfway down the calf (often made from worn out sails), a bright neckerchief (sometimes worn around the head), and a heavy, loose-fitting woolen shirt belted at the waist. Pirates often plastered their clothes with black tar to preserve them from the elements. This, as you can imagine, made them smell and feel terrible. Worse still, pirates wore no underwear and only occasionally washed their clothes in seawater, so you can imagine just how smelly and itchy they became after only a couple of weeks at sea.

By the Way

I bet you can't guess why pirates nearly always wore a large golden earring. It was so that if they ever drowned after a shipwreck, there'd be enough money to give them a decent burial (if their bodies turned up, that is).

Shoe-Free Zone

Ordinary pirates didn't generally like shoes. Firstly they usually couldn't afford them, having spent all their money on booze and gambling. Secondly, bare feet gave better grip on a deck covered in water (or—on a good day—blood), and were more practical for shinning up ropes, monkey fashion. Also, it must be said, the pirates did occasionally eat them if they became really desperate.

In the Mediterranean, where it got very hot, it was not unusual for the pirate crew to dispense with clothes altogether and swing about the rigging completely naked.

Time to Dress Up

When the pirate captains, surgeons, or quartermasters went ashore, they generally put on a kind of long, knee-length, brass-buttoned tunic, which they belted around the waist over long stockings or even tights. On their heads would be the famous tricorn hat and on their feet the highly fashionable, large-buckled, tallish-heeled shoes or boots.

During the sixteenth century, sailors usually wore slops. When they went ashore, they simply wore a tunic over them or tucked it into their slops like a shirt.

In those days, the captains often didn't look much more fashionable than anyone else when aboard ship, but whenever they went anywhere remotely special they dressed up to look like gentry, so everyone would know who they were dealing with. Most pirate captains insisted on wearing these magnificent clothes when they went into battle, and some even put them on when they were about to be hanged.

SHAME! HE ALWAYS LOOKS SO NICE!

Ruff Trade

In the 1500s, the time of Sir Francis Drake and Sir Walter Raleigh, a captain (even a pirate captain) would wear clothes consisting of breeches tied with colored ribbons around the knees, a padded doublet, heavily embroidered and with a scattering of jewels, one of those frilly collars around the neck, a voluminous cloak, and all of this finished off with a cocked hat with a big, brightly colored feather sticking out of it.

Just about everyone in those days had a beard and moustache (even some of the women, I wouldn't mind betting). Ordinary sailors would have their hair pulled back to keep it out of their eyes and plaited into a tarry pigtail. Pirates seldom cut their hair and were only forced to do so when it became inhabited by stowaway lice.

Seventeenth-Century Pirate Wear

In the 1600s, they still had the same baggy slops down to just below the knee, but this time with woollen stockings and a long shirt or coat. It was during this period that the extremely sissy-looking petticoat trousers became popular, especially with the captains. These looked like long, knee-length, wide-at-the-bottom divided skirts. The reason you don't see any of these outfits in pirate films is most likely because the directors don't want their heroes (or villains come to that) looking too girlish.

DARN. I'VE GOT A RUN IN ME STOCKING!

Cross-Dressing?

Talking of looking girlish, it was well recorded that when the rough and ragged pirates attacked a ship with ladies aboard, before doing anything else, they would rip off the poor damsels' clothes. Not, I must stress, to ogle at their naked bodies, or even to have their wicked way with them (that wasn't allowed)—but to steal their dresses. It was not that unusual to see a filthy, long-haired, tattooed, fully armed, macho pirate leaping around the deck wearing the latest in seventeenth-century high-court ladies' fashions.

SICK AS A PARROT

So here you have a relatively small ship in a relatively huge ocean inhabited by a relatively unruly bunch of shipmates. They not only didn't bathe properly, but didn't eat or drink well either. As a result, your bold buccaneer tended to be liable for just about every disgusting disease going. Not only that, but a lot of seamen picked up some very unpleasant illnesses from the brothels in ports visited on their travels.

WHO ARE YOU CALLING AN UNPLEASANT THING

And it wouldn't be down to the sickroom, where a nice nurse would tend to their every need—oh no! If your average pirate woke up feeling a little under the weather, there was a strong chance that he'd end up going over the side as fish food, for there was no such thing as a doctor aboard a pirate

ship (unless they'd captured one) let alone a nurse, and little in the way of medicine.

Sicknesswise, some places were worse than others. The pirates who hung around Europe and the cooler areas weren't at half the risk as those who sailed the tropics—those seas around the scorching, mosquito-infested coasts of Africa. Just as an example, seamen on the slave ships that plied the waters between Africa and the West Indies threw the corpses of four to five slaves overboard daily, as well as a fair proportion of their shipmates. It was much the same on the pirate ships. By the time a voyage was over, it was not unheard of for your average hardworking pirate to lose up to 40 percent of his friends.

So what were the main diseases?

Scurvy

Scurvy and seafaring men go together like dogs and fleas. This disease is reckoned to have killed 200,000 seamen between 1500 and 1900. The problem was dietary. Sailors didn't seem to realize that a human being needs fruits and vegetables to keep reasonably healthy. Even if they had realized it, however, in those days on board ship there was no way of keeping produce from rotting after more than a couple of days.

When your mom and dad tell you that you must eat your vegetables, they're not kidding (they're probably not pirates either, but we won't go into that). Scurvy is a nasty disease that results from a diet that includes no fruits or vegetables and therefore no vitamin C.

Symptoms

Loss of appetite, pale skin with dark blotches, spongy pimply gums that bleed easily, teeth falling out, swelling of the legs, roughness of the skin, diarrhea (even more unpleasant on a small ship with no bathrooms), awful lethargy, and a certain loss of vision. If you happen to have all these symptoms, might I suggest you go immediately to your local store and buy lots of lemons, limes, or oranges and suck 'em dry. It has been said that the symptoms will miraculously clear up in a couple of days—mine did!

Interesting Fact?

British sailors were called limeys because, after 1795, the Royal Navy provided fresh lime juice on all voyages. The British merchant navy followed in 1854. (The U.S. Navy didn't catch on until World War II.)

Yellow Fever

One of the bad things about living in and around a hot sunny climate like you get in Africa and the Caribbean is that you are far more likely to catch a horrid and scary disease called yellow fever. It was first "discovered" by the infamous sixteenth-century Spanish conquistadors when they conquered South America, and many say it served them right. You can lay the blame for us humans catching yellow fever fairly and squarely at the feet (all six of 'em) of your common mosquito and the forest monkeys from whom the skeeter picks up the disease.

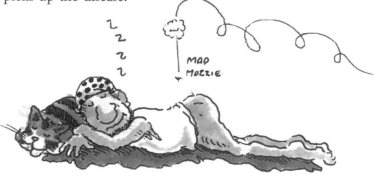

MAD MOZZIE

These days you'd be inoculated against it, but that option didn't exist around the seventeenth century. So if, in the middle of the night, your potential target pirate was to have a skeeter visitor, there was a fair chance that, providing the little varmint was carrying the disease, he'd get the full works. Which were:

Symptoms

For the first few days after being bitten, the patient could take it easy while the virus spread and multiplied throughout his body (yuck!). Then, suddenly, he'd get a chronic headache, backache, start being sick everywhere, and then he'd get hotter and hotter and HOTTER. After three long, sweat-pouring, hallucinating days of utter agony, his fever would go either of two ways. It could be:

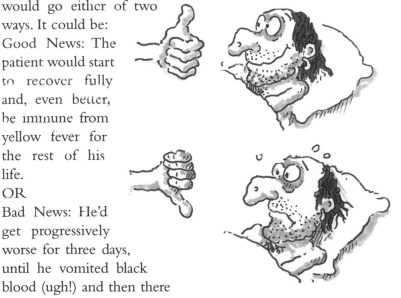

Good News: The patient would start to recover fully and, even better, be immune from yellow fever for the rest of his life.

OR

Bad News: He'd get progressively worse for three days, until he vomited black blood (ugh!) and then there wouldn't be any rest of his life. I suppose it wasn't all bad news; after all, he couldn't get the disease again either, could he?

Dysentery

Dysentery is a horrible disease and almost too yucky to talk about. You get it when a lot of people are crowded together, don't wash their hands after going to the bathroom, and then handle food. On a pirate ship, not only did they not have proper toilets (with soap dispensers and sinks, etc.), but the water was far too precious to be used for washing. Actually pirates were a filthy bunch who wouldn't have washed their hands anyway.

Symptoms

Don't worry, you'll soon know if you've got it: severe bouts of blood-filled diarrhea, followed by severe stomach pains, followed by a severe thirst, followed by, if you're a bit unlucky, severe death. Severely not to be recommended.

Medical Tip

If you've got dysentery, don't, for God's sake, confuse it with scurvy for, if you rush for the fruit bowl, it'll more than likely make it much worse.

Psittacosis (Parrot Disease)

Talk about "sick as a parrot." This is where the term comes from. Psittacosis is a nasty little disease of birds (particularly

SICK PARROT

parrots), which is easily transmitted to humans (particularly pirates). The joke is that the birds don't have that much of a bad time with the disease, but humans get it much worse (if you call dying much worse).

How to Catch it

Easy! Go to your parrot's cage, put your head through the door, and sniff the bottom (of the cage, not the parrot). Psittacosis is caught from inhaling the dust of dried-out parrot poop.

Symptoms

The patient starts climbing on people's shoulders, flapping his arms about, and copying everything they say at the top of his voice. Actually, that's a lie—it's worse than that. Someone with psittacosis suffers from an extremely high temperature of a hundred and something, followed by pneumonia, severe weakness, and really fast breathing. It lasts two to three weeks after which time he either gets better . . . or he doesn't!

By the Way

Pirates really did have parrots as pets, not always because they wanted them, but because the pesky peckers would often follow the pirate ships when they left their desert islands thinking there'd be more to eat. Often they'd be lucky if the pirates didn't eat them.

Injury Time

These days, if we hurt ourselves, we either search for a bandage, swallow an antibiotic or, if it's something more serious, call an ambulance and rush to the nearest hospital where a fully trained staff will figure out what's wrong (if you don't mind waiting). In the seventeenth century, there were no such things as hospitals, skilled surgeons, or drugs like antibiotics to combat infection. And that was on land! Ships, and especially pirate ships, were much, much worse, and so were the sorts of injuries pirates were likely to suffer. I mean, when did you last get hit on the back of the head

by a cannon ball or have your arm lopped off by
a cutlass?

Admittedly, on board ship, one of the crew would usually
be delegated to tend to the injured. But his equipment would
be primitive, to say the least, and although he'd more than
likely have his own sharp knives (essential pirate gear), for
major operations like amputations he'd simply borrow a saw
from the ship's carpenter—if indeed he wasn't the ship's
carpenter.

Anesthetic? Forget it. The patient would probably be filled
up with rum or brandy until sloshed to the point of oblivion.
This same alcohol would then be poured on the open wound
in a vain effort to ward off festering, but often with little
effect. One of the only ways of being sure of stopping the
infection was to put a lighted ember or red hot iron to the
injury (this was called cauterizing), but the patient had a nasty
habit of dying from the treatment, which was kind of
counterproductive. There is absolutely
no doubt that most of the
seamen who underwent any
form of surgery on pirate
ships would have died from
either the shock or the
infection that followed.
In fact, those guys
hobbling around on wooden
legs could be regarded as
the lucky ones.

THAT'S REALLY
LUCKY

Gangrene

Gangrene not only sounds disgusting, it is! It's a horrible disease that results from the infection that sets in after a severe wound or burn. This would have been the usual cause of death to most pirates after a battle at sea. The flesh actually begins to rot (especially in hot weather), owing to a lack of blood supply. The smell, as you can imagine . . . is—er—unimaginable. The only thing you can do is to keep cutting back behind the gangrene in the hope that the wound won't re-infect, but you can end up with no limb at all—which is a bit tricky if you're a pirate.

An Eye for an Eye

Pirates were very aware of the dangers of so much fighting and a proportion of any stolen haul was set aside by the quartermaster to compensate the men for any serious injury received in battle. It went like this:

- Worst of all was the loss of a right arm—the cutlass arm. For that, if he survived, he could expect 600 pieces of eight (Spanish dollars).
- The other arm or either leg came in slightly less at 500 pieces.
- A lost eye was worth 100 pieces of eight (which would buy a lot of black patches), but I suppose it's fair to surmise the loss of both would have been considerably more than double. Let's face it, there are better things to be than a pirate if you can't see.

Malaria

Anyone or anything can and could catch malaria—birds, monkeys, lizards, hamsters, pirates—and, of course, us. Just like yellow fever, it is carried by mosquitoes, but this time, there's sixty different types of the disease to choose from. Four of these affect humans: *Plasmodium vivax,* which causes the sufferer to have a fever every other day (only half as bad); *Plasmodium malariae,* which takes a long time to appear and causes fever every three days (only a third as bad); and the last two, *Plasmodium ovale,* which is mild, and *Plasmodium falciparum.* This last one gives you jungle fever and causes coma and madness and kills you pretty quickly by blocking the blood vessels to the brain (not that pirates had much brain to run blood vessels to).

Cure?

Ah, here lies the problem. Malaria is usually treated with quinine, a drug obtained from the bark of the cinchona tree. This is fine except the tree only grows in the Andean highlands of Peru—a slight problem if you're stuck in a boat miles from anywhere.

Consumption (Tuberculosis)

Very popular among those who live and work in cold, damp conditions with very poor food (in other words—pirate ships). This tricky little disease has a bad habit of lying around in the body for as long as it feels like before it decides to zap you. In fact, a quarter of us have the bacillus *Mycobacterium tuberculosis* lurking around inside us without our ever knowing.

Symptoms

Obviously, this sneaky disease shows no symptoms in the early stages (otherwise you'd know you had it), but after a while the patient starts feeling tired, feverish, loses his appetite, and begins to lose weight. Then, if it's the worst kind, he starts having chest pains and coughs up blood. If he doesn't get taken immediately to a hospital (which again is difficult if rocking about on the high seas) and isn't given a massive dose of antibiotics (not invented in those days), he usually dies—which most pirates had a habit of doing.

PUNISHING PIRATES

Almost all British pirates had at one time or another been in the Royal Navy or on merchant vessels—not by choice, but because they'd been "pressed" into it. The press-gang was feared by every hard-drinking man in every tavern in every port in the world. When a captain was a bit short in the old crew department for a particular voyage, he'd send out a bunch of his roughest, toughest men. Late in the evening, when most of the men in the taverns would be as drunk as parrots, the press-gang would grab as many as he needed. By the time the poor souls sobered up, it would be too late, they'd be at sea, and the only way back would be to swim.

By the Way

When a man joined the Royal Navy in those days, he'd receive a shilling from the king (rotten deal!). When a kidnapped seaman awoke aboard ship, he would find a shilling "pressed" in his hand. This was a slick trick to prove he'd agreed willingly.

Once at sea, that's when the trouble started. Discipline on board for your average seaman could be incredibly cruel. Disobedience could be punished in many ways. Sailors could be forced to swallow cockroaches, have their teeth knocked out, or have iron bolts screwed into their mouths so they'd choke on their own blood. Almost worst of all, they could be flogged by a frayed, tarred rope called a cat-o'-nine-tails while tied to the mainmast. Sometimes a man could be flogged over 500 times, and sometimes, just to add a little spice to the proceedings, the flogger would customize his whip by knotting the ends or adding musket balls or even fish hooks (ouch!). Then, if the floggee had been really disobedient, they'd rub salt and vinegar into his raw flesh after the event—guaranteed to make the poor fellow's eyes water even more.

Anyone for Keelhauling?

Then there was always keelhauling, the horrendous punishment by which the guilty party was dragged under and across the bottom of the ship by a rope so that the barnacles scraped his skin off—a punishment that was often fatal, especially if the victim got a severe nibbling by sharks.

All this for only a few bucks a month!

By the Way

In 1790 a lot of the worst punishments on British ships were banned when the Articles of War were published. (The articles were a serious and specific set of laws that all British sailors were expected to live by.)

Pirate Punishments

You could still be punished on pirate ships, but it generally wasn't quite so sadistic. Here are just a few examples:

Man Overboard

If a pirate was found guilty of a serious crime against another man, he'd either be thrown over the side and not thought of again or towed behind the ship on a length of rope until he was either dead from hypothermia (the cold), exhaustion, boredom, or simply drowning.

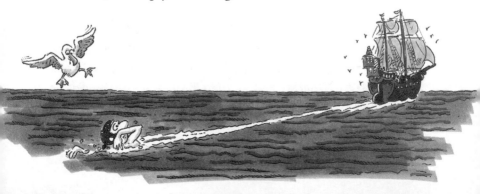

Marooning

If a crime wasn't quite so bad, but bad nonetheless, the pirates went in for marooning— that is, leaving the poor fellow on some remote, deserted island. Or they might set him adrift on just a tiny raft, with no clothes and no provisions (unless you count a gun to kill himself with if things started to look too dire). This was the punishment for anything approaching mutiny or threatening the captain.

Dunking

At suppertime this was quite often done to the hardtack to soften it and slightly less often to pirates who wouldn't do as they were told. They would lower the stubborn pirate over and over into the ocean and, in between, hang him up to dry in the blazing sun. Very good, as it happens, for the old suntan, but the victim very often ended up rather overdone.

Rules is Rules

Everyone thinks that being a pirate for a living meant that you didn't have to do all the stuff that real sailors had to do—wear pressed uniforms, brush your teeth, obey orders, bathe every night, not answer back to the captain, etc. But that was sometimes far from the truth. As you might imagine, having anything up to a couple of hundred rough, tough criminals on one ship could create a few problems. Pirates often had a strict set of rules to follow, and if they broke them, there'd be painful results.

Things Pirates Couldn't Do

Oddly enough, most pirate ships had a strict code of conduct, and this was often on display for all to see (and for all to sign). There were a few things that they just couldn't do— things like:

No Girls

Attempting to sneak women aboard, keeping them below decks, or even disguising them as regular seamen were all forbidden. If pirates were found to be doing this, the punishment was short and swift. They were either flung over the side (often in shark-infested waters), hung from the yard-arm, or simply run through with the captain's sword. Often pirates would be sailing for months or even years at a time. When they'd hit the seaports, they'd typically seek out brothels (whorehouses),

CAUSE AND EFFECT

where they often caught horrendous incurable diseases from the ladies of easy virtue.

45

It was forbidden to meddle with women of good birth from a captured ship. Penalty—DEATH. (It's usually thought that if pirates captured a ship, whatever was on board was theirs for the taking—including any women. Although they were generally allowed to have their will with the slaves and servant girls, they were strictly forbidden to ravage any of the high-born women—probably because the captain wanted them for himself!)

No Stealing

Anyone who stole anything over the value of a piece of eight (there was no such thing as a piece of seven) would be marooned on a desert island.

No Secrets

If a man tried to keep a big secret from the other pirates, he'd be sent away on a little raft with a small pistol, some powder, some shot, and a bottle of water if he was lucky.

No Violence

Any man who struck another on board and injured him could expect old Moses' eye-for-an-eye law—in this case thirty-nine lashes on his bare back.

No Dirty Weapons

If a man was found with a dirty weapon, if he was not ready at all times for service, or if he didn't do enough work around the place, he would forfeit his share of any stolen goods.

No Danger

If a man let off his musket for a laugh, or smoked his pipe down in the hold, or carried a candle without a cover, he also lost his share of any loot.

It Could Only Happen to Pirates (avoid this part if you're at all squeamish)

After all that stuff about the sort of treatment that sent sailors to become pirates, you might want to hear of some of the things they did to others when *they* were calling the shots.

Ups and Downs

When the British captain, William Snelgrave, was captured by pirates in 1719, he was forced to watch what they did to a French captain who'd been captured just before him. The pirates tied a rope round his neck and hoisted him up into the sails over and over again until he became unconscious. Another favorite was to stuff oakum (the tarry rope used for sealing the gaps between the ship's planks) into the mouths of their victims and then set fire to it.

No Sweat

A great pirate laugh was called "sweating," a fun little event in which the pirates would strip their victim and, to the tune of the ship's fiddler, force him to run around and around the mizzenmast by sticking him in the backside with knives, forks, harpoons, or anything sharp they could get their hands

on—until he collapsed from exhaustion. If the pirates felt that wasn't enough, they sometimes put the exhausted man into a barrel full of cockroaches who would gorge themselves on his blood. Nice!

Musical Cannons

There's a picture in *The Pirates* by Douglas Botting of two pirates in the year 1718 careering around the deck on the backs of a couple of Portuguese monks, whipping their steeds until the losers collapsed.

Woolding

You should have seen "woolding"—the old pirate method of finding out where the valuables were hidden. This sounds pretty innocent—like something you do to sheep—but it involved tying the victim's arms and legs with rope and stretching him while at the same time beating him with all kinds of implements. Then, just so he didn't get too cozy, he would have burning matches inserted between his fingers, or slender cords twisted about his head until his eyes burst out of his skull. I did warn you!

Barbecue Time

Sir Henry Morgan, who became the governor of Jamaica after a long career privateering, always made out he'd been pretty nice to his prisoners. Oh yeah! Not according to reports of what he did to the women of Portobelo when he captured the port in 1668. Apparently he threw them live onto a baking stove until well done, and all because he thought they had money, which of course they'd denied.

Blow Up

Then there were the buccaneers who tortured Dona Agustin de Rojas, probably the most important woman in Portobelo. She was stripped naked and forced into an empty wine barrel. The barrel was then filled all around her with gunpowder and a pirate held a lighted taper, far too close for comfort, while demanding the whereabouts of her valuables.

Around the Mast

But that was nothing! French pirate chief Montbars of Languedoc figured out a punishment all of his very own. Are you ready for this? He would slit open his victim's stomach and remove one end of his large intestine and nail it to a post. So far not so good. He would then force the victim to dance around and around the post by beating him with a burning spar until his guts (all twenty-five feet of them) were played out and he expired. Phew!

Sorry, folks, but even I can't describe what Captain Morgan's men did to the Portuguese after capturing Gibraltar, but it made the things that I've already described seem like a trip around Disneyland.

LADIES AT SEA

Don't go thinking there were only men out there on the high seas. Okay, being a pirate was generally thought of as a man's job, but there were several well-known female buccanesses throughout history. This is all the more amazing because most of the time women weren't allowed anywhere near pirate ships (unless they were captives or slaves).

All the famous women pirates had originally crept on board dressed as boys and, strange as it may seem, managed to hide their gender from their macho shipmates for quite a while. This was more difficult than you might think. All the guys on board the ships of the seventeenth and eighteenth centuries used to sleep together, eat together, use the same bathroom, and, much more to the point, bathe together—usually from a tub of water and usually on deck in front of everyone. More crucial than that, in hot weather pirates would often charge around in no clothes at all.

It might have escaped your notice, but men and women have a habit of being slightly different physically. Couple that with having no Adam's apple, no five o'clock stubble, no hairy chest— not to mention having a much higher voice, and it all becomes mystifying, to say the very least, how the women were never spotted.

Here are a few lady pirates who not only got away with it, but were eventually able to be recognized for who they really were.

Anne Bonny

Anne Bonny was born in Ireland in the late seventeenth century. She was the illegitimate daughter of a well-known Cork lawyer named William Cormac. His wife kicked him out of the house when she discovered that he'd been having an affair with the maid (who ended up in prison on a false robbery charge). Little Anne was the result of their "indiscretion".

Cormac, as it happens, was very fond of his daughter and decided that he'd like her to come and live with him, but he couldn't admit that she was actually his. He made out, therefore, that she was a boy and that he was simply training "him" as a clerk. To cut the story short, it all came out, and Anne's dad, along with Anne and the maid (now out of jail), sailed to America to start a new life.

But Anne was a wild child with a real sense of adventure and a talent for boxing, of all things. She got together with and married a young trainee pirate called James Bonny and together they sailed to the Bahamas to look for trouble. To cut the short story even shorter, she fell out with her husband and fell in with the swashbuckling "Calico" Jack Rackham, a much-hunted pirate captain. With him she stole a ship and started her true pirate career. But, as I said earlier, pirate ships didn't allow women, let alone wives, on board, so Anne simply reverted to what she knew best and masqueraded as a man again.

Mary Read

Mary Read was born in Britain toward the end of the seventeenth century. Due to a little misunderstanding, her mother's husband had run off to sea before Mary was born, leaving Mary's mother with a young son. Her mother then became pregnant again almost immediately by someone else and, just before the baby (Mary) was born, the son died (so far so bad). Then, to avoid admitting to an illegitimate child and so as to get money off her runaway husband's rich parents, Mary's mother moved away and made out that Mary was the baby boy who had died. From then on, therefore, Mary had to be male. Clear so far?

At thirteen, Mary got a job in a big London house as a footboy not a maid. But she found this boring and also ran away to sea like her mother's old husband, still dressed as a boy. After this, she joined the army, but carelessly fell in love with a boy (there's always a catch somewhere), who, as you might imagine, at first thought her behavior kind of strange until Mary revealed her true identity.

FONNY FELLOW!

Anyway, they left the army and started a pub together, but hubby carelessly died. In 1697 Mary, who wasn't really cut out for pub life, put on men's clothes once more, became a soldier again, and was posted to the West Indies. Guess what? The ship was captured by pirates and our Mary found herself in the same crew with Rackham and the other man/woman—Anne Bonny. Oh dear, oh dear, Anne Bonny found herself attracted to the dashing young "man," and eventually it became necessary for Mary and Anne to "compare notes," so to speak. Anne then confessed all to her husband Calico Jack Rackham, who told them both, for heaven's sake, to keep the fact that they were women under their hats (and their shirts). But then Mary suddenly fell for a fellow pirate and revealed all.

The two women, always dressed as men, were a formidable team, however. And were every bit as fierce and fearless as the rest of the crew. In 1720, after a short career of severe swashbuckling, when anchored off the island of Jamaica, Rackham and his merry men (and two women) were suddenly attacked by a British naval sloop. Rackham and the men were below decks lying around in a drunken stupor after a heavy night, so the two women fought the navy single-handedly with anything they could lay their hands on. They were magnificent. Eventually, however, when even *they* realized the game was up, they turned on their shipmates, who were now hiding below, calling them all cowards and killing and injuring several.

When Rackham and the rest of the crew were finally executed in Jamaica, Mary and Anne, also accused of "Piracies, Felonies, and Robberies . . . on the High Sea," were found guilty but got off on a technicality. While awaiting trial, they cleverly wheedled themselves into pregnancy, and it was the rule in those days that pregnant women could not be hanged—neat, eh?

By the Way

Just to prove what a toughie Anne Bonny was, when visiting her husband Calico Jack waiting for execution, she told him that she was admittedly sorry to see him in such a predicament but that if he'd fought like a man, he wouldn't be about to be hanged like a dog (who hangs dogs anyway, I ask myself?).

And later?

Mary died shortly after, before the birth of her baby, having caught the dreaded yellow fever in jail. It was rumored that Anne's wealthy dad (remember him?) bought his daughter's release.

Grace O'Malley

If you're one of those people who's interested in buried treasure and stuff like that, you might be interested in Grace O'Malley, the sixteenth-century Irish pirate who apparently buried nine tons of it. But before you go out with your bucket and shovel, beware . . . Old Grace apparently laid a nasty curse on anyone who should happen to find it. (Mean or what?)

Grace O'Malley came from the mighty and powerful O'Malley family, which had forts and castles all over the western coast of Ireland, as well as a huge fleet of pirate ships. Grace, by the way, when a little girl, was horribly scarred on the face by the beak and talons of a naughty eagle, whom she was trying to dissuade from carrying off her daddy's lambs.

Anyway, Mr. O'Malley trained his daughter to be a brave warrior(ess), and, when he died, she took over as leader of the terrifying O'Malley pirates, who caused havoc all along the coast of Ireland. So much so that Queen Elizabeth I, who ruled England from 1558 to 1603, offered the equivalent of $120,000 for her capture.

Grace really was some girl by all accounts, and there are hundreds of legends and stories about her bravery. Apparently, when she was a young mother (her son was one day old), she helped repel some Muslim pirates who were attacking her ship. Her captain supposedly came below to report that they were getting the worst of it. Grace cursed her crew and rushed onto the deck with a musket in one hand and presumably the baby in the other shouting and screaming fit to frighten the very bravest Muslim.

Later, when sixty years old, she attacked a Spanish vessel just off the coast of Ireland, this time crashing onto the deck in her nightie, waving her pistols, and looking fierce in her curlers and all. The poor Spaniards thought Grace was a crazed ghost and surrendered without firing a shot.

By the Way

As a caring parent, it must be said, the old girl left a lot to be desired. Legend has it that on one occasion her poor son fell overboard while they were on their way home after a few weeks' persistent pirating. He eventually struggled to the side of the boat and grabbed at it, but his mother chopped off his hand, leaving him to die in the waves claiming that had he been a true O'Malley, he wouldn't have fallen over in the first place. A hard way to learn a lesson, I'd have thought! Grace was eventually captured but, after an eighteen-month stretch in a Limerick jail, soon returned to her old tricks again. In the meantime, her hubbie had died. In those days, a wife had no right to her husband's lands, so Grace found herself alone and vulnerable. Instead of waiting to be attacked by her hostile neighbors, old Grace attacked them first. She was captured yet again, and this time her whole fleet was confiscated. But Grace appealed to Queen Elizabeth as one woman to another, claiming she'd been forced into it. Queen Liz rather liked the eccentric old girl and ordered her captors to figure it all out, to give Grace a break, and to let her live the rest of her life in comfort and peace. The old pirate died aged seventy-three in 1603, and one of her brave sons went on to become Viscount Mayo.

Mrs. Cheng

To be honest, there were quite a few girl/boys like the ones I've just mentioned, but you couldn't really beat the infamous Chinese pirate chief Cheng I Sao. Mrs. Cheng, as she was known, was a Chinese prostitute from

Canton (now called Guangzhou) and the widow of Cheng I who'd controlled all the sea between Hong Kong and Vietnam. They ruled an army of the most bloodthirsty pirates ever to sail the seven seas.

Nothing was safe from Mr. and Mrs. Cheng. They even ran a protection racket for the smaller merchant ships, which they couldn't be bothered to plunder, as well as all the little fishing vessels that operated in the same waters. The merchants were forced to pay fees at a series of collection posts along the coast.

Mr. Cheng died violently in 1807, and his wife promptly appointed Chang Pao, a brilliant buccaneer whom her husband had once captured and later adopted, to command what she called the Red Flag Fleet. She had an affair with him and later married him. While Mrs. Cheng remained the total boss, Chang became in charge of operations. Their house (or boat) rules were even stricter than those of the Caribbean pirates and went along these lines:

1) Rape of women prisoners was punished by death, but if—and here's the rub—the woman in question had agreed to it, it was still off with the head for the man, and over the side for the woman (with a heavy weight tied to her ankles).

2) For disobeying orders or stealing any of the treasure before it was shared, instant beheading.

3) Desertion or absence without leave was met with a severe loss in the ear department (both were chopped off).

4) If plundered goods were concealed, it was a whipping of the worst order, and on a second offense—it was severe head removal again (well not actually again, but you know what I mean).

Mrs. Cheng became so powerful that even the Chinese army and navy couldn't get near her. She had nearly 400 oceangoing junks, larger than many a countrys' navy and at times up to 7,000 men. And, oh boy, was she cruel. At one time in 1809, her boys attacked a village that had helped her enemies, and took horrible revenge. They burned it to the ground and beheaded its eighty male inhabitants, hanging their heads on a large banyan tree as a warning to others. The women and children were dragged off to the boats to be done with as Mrs. Cheng saw fit.

In the end, the Chinese asked for the help of the British and Portuguese navies. But even that didn't work—the pirates were just too powerful. So the Chinese government offered Cheng and Chang an amnesty (basically if they promised to be good right away, they'd be free from prosecution).

Mrs. Cheng and Chang Pao liked the idea and settled down in Canton, where the former opened a Chinese restaurant—no she didn't, she opened a massive gambling house and died, aged sixty-nine, an immensely rich old lady.

PIRATE FUN

Being a pirate wasn't all about capturing treasure ships, swigging grog, counting treasure, and stuff like that. Much of the time was spent lounging around on deck, desperate for something to come over the horizon that they could attack. Pirate ships, if you think about it, weren't often actually going anywhere, so they'd loiter around the trade routes waiting for ships that actually were. Sometimes they could hang around for months and therefore had to amuse themselves as best they could. Here are a few of the things they got up to:

Heads You Win

Pirates loved to gamble with cards, dice, or even who they were going to capture next. In fact, gambling was almost as popular as drinking (well almost). One of the problems was that pirates being pirates, they could get completely carried away and lose all their property, not to mention the clothes they stood up in or even their wives back home. And, almost inevitably, just like in the cowboy films, it would all end in a massive fight. Many captains, like privateer Woodes Rogers, actually had to ban gambling of any kind on board his ship, the *Duke*. He made everyone, right down to the cabin boy's parrot, sign a document, in case they changed their minds.

PIRATE PANTS

Some captains who didn't actually ban gambling were often able to use the sailors' inability to control their weakness to their advantage. You see, the trouble with big pirate ships (just like small kids) had always been that when the crew wanted to go ashore for fun and games, someone had to stay behind to look after the ship. Obviously all those who had lost their hard-fought-for money had to stay aboard, while the others hit the town.

Mock Trials

Most pirates, despite being a bloodthirsty lot, were pretty scared of the prospect of what would happen to them if they ever got caught—a quickish trial, a tallish gibbet, and a longish rope—and that's if they were lucky! It became quite common to act out a mock trial, a weird kind of pantomime where everyone aboard dressed up for his part. The captain was usually the judge, and the rest of the crew would play the lawyers, the jury, the jailer and, would you believe it, the hangman. In this way, they were able to make light of their almost inevitable fate—to spit in its face, so to speak.

DID ANYONE PACK THE SCRABBLE?

These trials were often acted out with such reality that the poor accused (usually not the brightest member of the crew) became genuinely scared for his life. On one occasion in 1717, a young pirate got himself so wound up that he thought his fellow shipmates really were going to hang him. He lost the plot so badly, in fact, that he threw a homemade grenade at the mock jury and then drew his cutlass and hacked off the arm of the guy acting as the prosecuting lawyer—a pirate who went by the name of Alexander the Great (from then on presumably, Alexander the One-Armed Great).

Party Time

Every time pirates overhauled a ship, they'd have a wild party when they got back to their own boat. As we've already established, they loved to imbibe and were crazy about drinking toasts to just about anyone they could think of— their wives, mistresses, friends, parrots, shipmates, past conquests, future conquests—you name it. Some of the most popular toasts were to God or the Devil, or death to any of a whole gaggle of judges, naval captains, or even royalty who were after their greasy necks. It is said that on the pirate island of Madagascar in the Indian Ocean the speciality was to mix gunpowder with the rum for specially solemn oaths and toasts. Madagascar, by the way, was almost exclusively a pirate island from the 1680s right into the eighteenth century, and many of the leaders had private armies surrounding their massive fortresslike houses.

There were, in fact, many pirate havens where like-minded villains could relax and party to their heart's content with their feet firmly on dry land. The pirates tended to favor tricky little harbors into which huge ships couldn't follow them. The ports—places like Tortuga Island near Hispaniola, New Providence Island in the Bahamas, the Juan Fernández Islands near Chile, Devil's Island off northern South America, and Ocracoke Island on the North Carolina coast—were chosen by their nearness to the trade routes and their faraway-ness from the powers that were out to get them. But their real favorites were the corrupt ports that operated outside the law and actually encouraged the pirates' lucrative business—Port Royal in Jamaica, Algiers on the North African coast, and Fort Dauphine on Madagascar, for example.

Pirate Music

Music was essential to keep pirates' spirits up. Most naval and merchant captains would insist on a ship's band or even a small orchestra. There's no reason to suppose that pirate ships didn't do the same. We know, for instance, that one of the most-prized treasures to be removed from a conquered ship (after the carpenter and the surgeon) would be anyone who could play a musical instrument like a fiddle or a squeeze-box.

These musicians often didn't mind being captured that much, because without doubt, their duties on a pirate ship would be much lighter. And let's face it, being captured was an almost watertight defense if they ever came to trial.

Music While You Work

There would be music while the crew ate their supper, scrubbed the deck, spliced the main brace, shivered their timbers, and most evenings before bedtime. And then there were the dances.

YOU DANCE DIVINELY

Pirates loved to dance and thought nothing of getting up and dancing with each other to the hornpipe or jig. Best of all, the ship's band would play rousing battle songs while the rest of the pirates were chasing and attacking other boats— banging drums and crashing cymbals and generally making a god-awful noise simply to scare the wits out of their prospective victims.

Many of the pirates' shanties are far too crude to share here, and they mostly boast about pirate exploits not only when fighting but with the opposite sex. Others were sad, whiney laments about their sweethearts back home or what was going to happen to them if they ever got caught.

THE PICK OF THE BUNCH

There were thousands of pirates terrorizing the seven seas during the seventeenth and eighteenth centuries, but some stood out head and shoulders above the rest. Here's the pick of the best—or worst—of 'em!

Blackbeard—The Weirdest

Blackbeard was the nickname given to a dangerous guy named Edward Teach, who was born in Bristol, England, sometime in the late seventeenth century. In a way, he was a failed sailor who turned lawbreaker because he wasn't getting anywhere in the Royal Navy. Nonetheless, he gained a reputation as one of the most terrifying of all pirates and is still more talked about than any of the famous naval captains of the day. Here are just a few of the stories about the old devil.

Appearance

Not content with being fierce, Blackbeard had to *look* fierce as well. He had a good start, for he was built like a wrestler with a horribly twisted nose and big ears. He added to this by sporting a huge, shaggy beard (black obviously), which he

wore in filthy ringlets. To set all this off, Blackbeard would wear a black wide-brimmed pirate hat pulled down right to his eyes. Best of all, when in fighting mode, he would weave hemp cords soaked in saltpeter and limewater into his hair and beard and light them. In doing so, he'd surround his massive head with an eerie glow and thick black smoke.

His demonic appearance was accompanied by a shoulder belt of pistols ready for action and a waist belt with even more pistols and various dangerous-looking daggers and cutlasses. Not someone you'd want to meet on a dark night in a small boat, I'll wager.

Fun and Games

In order to show his crew who was boss, Blackbeard would think up crazy tests of bravery and endurance. Like creating a "hell" of his very own, which he did by challenging his toughest sailors to accompany him down below, where he battened down all the hatches and lit pots of lethal brimstone. As the choking yellow fumes filled the pirates' parlor, one by one the crew dashed on deck gasping in the fresh air, while Blackbeard remained laughing belowdecks.

Gaining Respect

Another time, he was sitting at a table, down below, having a pleasant after-work drink with his shipmates, when he suddenly blew out the candles and pulled out his two huge pistols. Before anyone could get a word out, he shot right under the table, smashing the knee of Israel Hands, his second in command, who was taken immediately to the wooden leg department.

When the others rather falteringly asked why exactly he'd done it, Blackbeard replied quite calmly that if he didn't shoot one of his crew every now and again, they might forget exactly who he was—which is fair enough, I suppose.

Caution

Further research suggests that some of these stories are exaggeratons—made up by the great novelist and historian (and fibber) Daniel Defoe (who'd say anything to sell a few more books). True, Edward Teach, alias Blackbeard, was very much on the wrong side of respectability. And true you wouldn't want him to marry your sister, but there is no documented record of his ever really killing or torturing anyone for a laugh.

But, nonetheless, he did commit some gross acts of piracy, did cheat his crew out of most of their share of the bounty, and did manage to die in the most spectacular manner.

Blackbeard Backs Out—Ungracefully

On November 17, 1718, two naval sloops sailed south to capture Edward Teach who by now had a hefty price (and his famous wide-brimmed hat) on his head. They caught up with him five days later at the Ocracoke Inlet, North Carolina— the old blackguard's favorite hideout. When Blackbeard realized who they were, he laughed heartily, downed a huge tankard of rum, and yelled across to the officers on the other boat: "Damnation to anyone who should give or ask quarter [mercy]." Which was pretty rude, you must admit.

Young Lieutenant Robert Maynard, who was in command of one of the naval sloops, shouted back, "I shall expect no quarter from you and shall give none." Fighting talk in anyone's language.

After an all-out fight between the ships, the two captains finally came face to horrible face on Maynard's deck, which Blackbeard and his merry men had boarded without so much as an invitation. First they fought with pistols. Blackbeard's missed due to his inebriated state, but Maynard's hit home, unfortunately having absolutely no effect whatsoever. Then, just like in the movies, it was cutlasses. They fought hard until poor Maynard's blade was broken in two. Then, just as Maynard stepped back to cock his other pistol, Blackbeard lumbered forward for the kill. Unfortunately (for Blackbeard), a naval seaman jumped in his way and slashed him right across the throat as he passed, causing him to spout a frothy fountain of blood and generally make a terrible mess everywhere. The brave lieutenant, now ready, managed to shoot Blackbeard again but, once more, it didn't stop him. But another slash from a broadsword right across the back of his neck did. (I'm surprised his head didn't fall right off.) Well, it did stop him, but it still didn't bring him down. The old sea dog, bleeding and cursing, wavered for what seemed a long time trying desperately to cock another of his many pistols. Eventually, however, he crashed, like a bewildered bull in a bullring, to the blood-soaked deck—stone cold dead. When they finally examined his body, they found twenty-five separate wounds. All the other pirates, by the way, either surrendered or dived over the sides before you could say "shiver my timbers."

They hadn't even waited to see the boss's huge head finally being severed from his huge body and stuck triumphantly on the front of Maynard's sloop as a grisly trophy.

Bartholomew Roberts—The Cleverest

Welshman Bartholemew Roberts, born in 1682, had been an honest, hardworking seaman both in the Royal Navy and on merchant ships for more than thirty years. He was a natural sailor but realized, like Blackbeard, that his dream of becoming a captain was never going to happen—certainly not on the right side of the law.

His life of villainy started almost by accident. He was second mate on a slave ship called the *Princess* when it (and he) were captured by another Welshman, pirate captain Howell Davis in his ship the *Rover*. Davis actually liked Roberts but couldn't persuade him to join in the pirate fun. It was only when Davis was shot dead during a daring raid that the swarthy crew asked Bartholomew if he'd like to be their captain (they hadn't any idea how to sail the silly boat). Forget this thing about being a prisoner for an adventure, Roberts thought, and decided to reject king and country and accept the generous offer. Let's face it, if you're going to be a pirate, you might as well be the captain!

Bartholomew Roberts or Black Bart (as he was soon nicknamed) was to become probably the greatest pirate captain ever. There was no more spectacular mariner to be found in all the seven seas, and no one was more flamboyant. In his red vest and breeches, a red feather stuck in his tricorn, wearing a flashy diamond cross on a thick gold chain and two pairs of pistols hanging off a red silk sling over his shoulders, he was a brilliant sight.

On his first trip, he struck gold—literally—running into a fleet of forty-two Portuguese ships parked in the harbor of Bahia (now Salvador) on the Brazilian coast, waiting for an armed escort. The first boat they attacked turned out to be the richest, and Black Bart and his crew escaped with a haul of 90,000 gold moidores and chests of fabulous jewelry. The

BARTHOLOMEW ROBERTS

latter included that priceless diamond cross specially made for the king of Portugal, which the pirate captain was to wear at all times. Almost best of all the loot were the bales of fine tobacco. Not a shot had been fired.

Black Bart was an extraordinary fellow, being very cruel on the one hand but terribly fair on the other. His code of rules on board ship was designed so that each man should be treated equally and honestly—odd on a ship whose sole purpose was to rob and kill with maximum barbarity.

Bart's Rules (well, some of them):

- All candles were to be out by eight o'clock—bedtime. Anyone who wanted to carry on drinking had to do it on deck—and quietly.

- No fighting allowed on board. All arguments were to be settled on land under the supervision of the quartermaster. The rivals were first asked to fight a duel with pistols. If they both missed, they switched to swords. The winner was the first to draw blood.
- No gambling or women were allowed on board. Women prisoners were protected by armed guards.

On one occasion, when mildly insulted by a drunken crew member, Roberts ran the poor guy through with his sword on the spot. Someone else in the crew, a fellow called Jones, yet another Welshman, thought this unfair and had the nerve to curse the captain and attack him, throwing him clean over a cannon. A mini-mutiny looked imminent, but, at the quartermaster's quickly convened inquiry, it was decided for the whole business to work (being pirates and all), that the captain must be respected and obeyed at all times and that Jones should have two lashes of the cat-o'-nine-tails from

121-OUCH! -122-OUCH!
-123-OUCH!-
124-OUCH!-
125-OUCH!-
126....

each member of the crew. This normally wouldn't have been so bad, but at that time there were 180 of 'em.

On another occasion in 1722, when one of eleven British slave ships failed to surrender, Roberts's crew poured tar over the deck and set fire to the ship with eighty slaves on board, still chained together in pairs. This created a huge problem for the victims. They could either leap over the side and be lunch (double portion) for the sharks that were waiting in the surrounding waters or stay to be roasted alive. What a choice!

Black Bart and his crew of sixty were to become legendary throughout the Caribbean and around the African coast for their sheer nerve and stupendous sailing ability, at times attacking up to twenty-six ships at a time.

Vendetta

Roberts had a fixation about sailors from either of the islands of Martinique or Barbados because of their governors' constant and annoying attempts to catch him. If he ever captured any pirates from these two island nations, he would either cat-o'-nine-tail them almost to a pulp, cut off their ears, or tie them to the mainmast and use them for target practice. (Not their ears—the sailors!) Once, when capturing a ship sailing out of Martinique, Roberts discovered to his great glee that the ship was carrying the island's governor. Black Bart thought it a great joke to have him hanged from the yardarm and left dangling there for the rest of the trip.

Roberts died as he had lived, attacking a far stronger naval vessel, the *Swallow*, that had been trying for eight months to catch him. The brave buccaneer, not yet forty, had his throat ripped open by some stray grapeshot. His crew were instantly broken and disillusioned without him (some even cried out loud—big sissies) and were soon captured. Actually it was later revealed that most of them were still drunk from the merriment of the night before and couldn't have fought to save their miserable lives. Many of those captured, unfortunately (depending on which way you look at it), died on their way to trial, but it would hardly have done them any good if they hadn't, for, all in all, fifty-two were hanged and eighteen of the very worst were cut down, tarred, and hung in cages from gibbets till they eventually rotted right down to their bare bones.

Edward (Ned) Low—The Cruelest

Another brilliant mariner, Edward Low, was a Londoner, born at the beginning of the eighteenth century. As a boy, he couldn't read or write and made a living by stealing coins off other boys and beating them up if they objected. As a youngster, he immigrated to Boston, Massachusetts, and began work as a ship rigger (the only honest thing he ever did) before going to sea in 1721. Low soon disagreed with his first captain and even fired a shot at him. Luckily it missed, but unluckily it blew the brains out of another crew member who was carelessly standing behind him.

WHOOPS— SORRY!

Low stole the small boat that the crew used to go to shore and, with a few shipmates, took off, captured a ship, and headed for Jamaica, where they ran up a black flag and decided to try piracy. It became his chosen calling, and before long he was plundering numerous ships and having success throughout the Caribbean. But all this was kids' stuff, and Low eventually captured a magnificent schooner that he took a fancy to and appropriately called her the *Fancy*. He then hired more men and went pirating in earnest.

His reputation grew within a year, not only for the boats he robbed, but for the enormous cruelty he used while doing it. The stories of his barbarity are legendary, especially against the Spaniards and the French, whom he hated. At one time, he overtook a Spanish privateer and on examination discovered it had taken prisoner a group of captains from recently overhauled American ships. Low wasn't wild about Americans at the best of times, but at least they weren't Spaniards. On the basis of the old pirate saying—"dead men tell no tales"—he promptly slaughtered everyone aboard. Any that went over the side in terror were relentlessly pursued in boats and clubbed senseless as they tried to swim for safety. He then burned the ship and sank her.

Admiral Low (as he eventually called himself) wasn't an admirer of the Portuguese either. He once took a Portuguese ship on its way home from Brazil with a fortune in gold on board. Well, not actually on board. The captain had hung the coins in a large sack outside his cabin window. When he saw the pirate ship bearing down on him, he cut the sack loose and let it sink to the bottom of the ocean (where it presumably still is). For this Mr. Low cut off the captain's lips, boiled them in oil, and then murdered his thirty-two shipmates in front of him. That must really redefine "angry."

At the end of his career, when he was on the run from HMS *Greyhound*, he became so furious at the ship's persistence that he decided to take it out on anyone he came across. First to come along was a large whaling sloop. For no good reason, he stripped the poor captain naked and cut off his ears before shooting him through the head (at least he couldn't hear the bang!). Then, again for no reason, he sent the poor crew off in a little whaling boat with nothing more than a couple of dry biscuits, some water, and a compass. But worse was still to come. A day or so later, he took the captains of two more whaling boats on board his ship. He disemboweled one of them, then took out his heart, cooked it, and forced one of his crew to eat it. The other one was

slashed mercilessly, before being made to eat his own ears, which had been roasted but luckily sprinkled with salt and pepper (unfortunately ketchup hadn't been invented). There's no record of the poor unfortunate not enjoying the meal, but they do say he died later of his injuries.

Eventually, Low was set upon by his crew for murdering the quartermaster in his sleep after an argument, and was put overboard with a couple of his shipmates in a little boat with no provisions. They were in luck—well, sort of. They were picked up by a ship shortly afterward. But it was a French ship (the French were after Low and company even more than anyone else). The French crew threw him and his shipmates in irons and took them off to Martinique, where they were tried and then hanged for crimes against humanity. Or were they? Some historians tell another story—that Low escaped and disappeared off the face of the earth.

Henry Morgan—The Most Successful

Yet *another* Welshman (I give up), Henry Morgan, was born in 1635 into a well-to-do military family. Henry wanted to be a soldier and joined the expeditionary force of 7,000 troops sent to capture the Spanish stronghold of Hispaniola. When that didn't work, he decided to attack Jamaica, which turned out to be an easy target.

Gradually Morgan got to lead his own raids on

CAPTAIN MORGAN

Jamaica, and he gained great fame as one of the most fierce and feared enemies of the Spaniards. When Edward Mansfield, the leader of the privateers (respectable pirates), was executed by the Spaniards, Morgan was chosen to replace him. Thus, at only thirty-two, he became admiral of the Brethren of the Coast, a wily band of buccaneers and ill-disguised cutthroat pirates. Their greatest coup was to capture the Spanish stronghold and largest port in South America, Portobelo, against ridiculous odds. He then sent a snide letter to the Spanish governor saying he could have his town back for a ton of money or Morgan would burn the place to the ground. After much toing and froing, Morgan walked (or sailed) away with a hefty treasure in gold coins, silver bars, and chests chock-full of silver plate. Everyone back home in Britain was overjoyed, and Morgan was an overnight superhero. But by now Henry had got the taste for money and was soon out aplundering once more.

Got a Light?

After one such raid, Morgan and his boys celebrated so hard and became so drunk that someone accidentally dropped a lighted something or other near the gunpowder supply, and the whole ship was blown to smithereens. Our Henry, lucky as ever, was picked up in the sea, a trifle damp but otherwise okay—one of only ten survivors.

Captain Henry Morgan went on to wreak more havoc among the Spaniards, but as he did so he gained a reputation for cruelty far beyond what was necessary. His destruction of Panama City went down in history as an orgy of looting, killing, and torture that has seldom been equaled. More to the point, many of his attacks occurred after a peace treaty had already been signed between Britain and Spain, a fact that naturally got him into deep trouble. Also, he was terribly unfair when it came to sharing the spoils with his crew, always taking the lion's share for himself.

Despite all this, the admittedly brave captain still led a charmed life and was knighted in 1674 and sent back to Jamaica as its lieutenant governor. The ultimate joke was that in the following years, until his death in 1668, the fabulously wealthy Sir Henry Morgan spent most of his time suppressing buccaneering and piracy, hanging hundreds of his former colleagues and associates. All this was ironic—not to mention two-faced—when you come to think of it.

God Speaks?

In 1692 Port Royal, reputedly the most wicked town in the Western Hemisphere, was destroyed by a massive earthquake, burying forever the tomb of the notorious and illustrious Henry Morgan.

Stede Bonnet—The Most Cultured

Major Stede Bonnet was different from all the other pirates and buccaneers. Born in 1688, he became a respected, educated, and extremely cultured man of letters and went into piracy merely to get away from his missus whose nagging was driving him around the bend (or out to sea). Bonnet had owned a substantial sugar plantation on the island of Barbados until, suddenly, without warning and knowing about as much as you or I do about the sea, disappeared. Secretly, he'd fitted out a fast sloop, which he called the *Revenge*, with ten guns and an extensive library of his favorite books, had assembled a crew of seventy similarly minded men and then simply sailed off into the sunset to look for fame and fortune—brilliant stuff! And wasn't he good at it. After lots of fun on the high seas, he eventually ended up in the same raiding group as Blackbeard. Along with the *Revenge* (now sporting thirty guns and a crew of 300), he became, like Edward Teach, a big name in the world of piracy. The debonair major, by the way, took no part in the actual sailing but strolled the deck in a silk morning gown, drink in one hand and one of his many volumes in the other.

Later on, a contrite Bonnet managed to sweet-talk his way into a pardon for his dastardly deeds and was even given a privateer's commission to act against the Spaniards (he could now rob, murder, and pillage legally). But the miffed major had a few old scores to settle with Blackbeard, who'd cheated him out of a large share of loot. So, instead of going after the Spaniards, like he'd promised, he set out in the opposite direction to chase the old dog down. He soon forgot all about privateering. Changing his name to Captain Roberts and his sloop's to the *Royal James*, he started robbing and looting with new passion.

Bonnet (alias Roberts) was eventually captured after a long, bloodthirsty, and spectacular chase, and he and his men were brought to Charleston for trial. At the trial, the judge really let Bonnet have it for committing eleven acts of piracy after he'd been pardoned for killing eighteen naval men who'd been sent to get him. Bonnet was apparently shocked at the death sentence and was taken groveling, posy in hand, and making an awful fuss, to be hanged with the rest of his men at a special gallows in Charleston Harbor.

IT WASN'T ME. HONEST!

François L'Olonnois—The All-around Nastiest

There's bad pirates, there's very bad pirates, and then, way out in front in the badness stakes there's François L'Olonnois. Born Jean David Nau, at the back end of the seventeenth century, he started life as a lowly bonded servant on one of the West Indian islands before moving to the pirate island of Hispaniola. He then became one of the early boucaniers. Then he joined with others to start real buccaneering, first from canoes and then from small ships that they captured. The young Frenchman was noted for his almost lunatic courage and was soon given a commission to try to take the big Spanish treasure ships.

After many hair-raising adventures, he was eventually reported dead to the governor of Cuba. But the wily old governor didn't believe it and sent a posse of ships to track him down. They eventually did.

But it all ended up with L'Olonnois, on board the ship that had been attacking him, personally chopping off the heads, one by one, of all those who'd hidden below decks, as they poked their heads out to see what was going on. All except one, who was spared simply so he could report back to the governor.

The vicious pirate's small armada gradually grew to eight separate ships with 700 men, and together they robbed and plundered and murdered as far as Mexico and Nicaragua. They looted small coastal cities to the tune of 260,000 pieces of eight. The stories of their cruel and unrelenting torture almost defy belief.

As an example, when a prisoner claimed he didn't know the route to his hometown, which L'Olonnois was trying to reach and plunder, the monster ripped him open, tore out his heart, chewed on it, and then threw it in the face of his friend saying that he'd do the same to him if he didn't play ball.

Eventually, by poetic justice, L'Olonnois himself was captured by a band of grumpy Indians, who took great delight in hacking him limb from limb, cooking him in a big pot, and then eating him for supper.

HANGING AROUND

If piracy had become your chosen profession, it was generally regarded as a bad idea to get caught. Then as now, any kind of illegal behavior on the high seas was likely to make the powers-that-be (or were) very annoyed. In the pirates' and mutineers' cases, the trial was generally an open and shut one—no warnings, reprimands, or light fines, etc. The penalty—death by public hanging—was almost inevitable. London was a favorite place for hanging, particularly in the neighborhood of Wapping—a murky, smelly, labyrinth of docks, gin shops, wharves, alehouses, brothels, and boat builders, all crammed together in a tangle of rope-strewn masts.

Between Wapping New Stairs and King Henry's Stairs, as they are called today, was the notorious Execution Dock, a gallows designed purely for punishing pirates. These unfortunates were destined to "dance the hempen jig" on a rope just above the waterline at low tide. There they would be hanged pathetically just above the oozing mud, as the filthy Thames River covered their limp bodies for three tides—a symbol of the jurisdiction of Britain's Lord High Admiral. He was the guy whose job it was to oversee the punishment of all those who did their dirty deeds on the high seas and waterways up to low tide mark. Crimes committed above the tide mark were tried by the civil courts. On the other side of the river, built on piles, stood the ancient Angel Inn, where that old tyrant Judge George Jeffreys (the hanging judge) would sit having a quiet drink while watching his condemned subjects being "turned off," as he so charmingly put it, across the water (beats darts, I suppose).

Up until 1723, only the captain and the quartermaster of a pirate ship would have actually been hanged, but the war against piracy became so frenzied that it was decided to string up anyone who'd even sniffed a pirate boat, let alone sailed under the Jolly Roger. Except, of course, for those who'd been captured at sea and forced into it. Needless to say, the most common defense of your average accused pirate was that he had been made to sign the pirates' articles (and who can blame him), but they seldom got away with their crimes because they were usually incriminated by the ones who'd already been told they were going to swing. Others swore blind that they knew the whereabouts of lots of other pirates and would help track them down if their lives were spared. There really is no honor among thieves or pirates.

THICK AS A PIRATE ↓

Execution Day

An execution was a fun day out for the average London family in the sixteenth and seventeenth centuries. And the demise of a dastardly pirate was probably the best gig of all. Hours before it happened, crowds would arrive at Execution Dock from both sides of the river—at that time it was relatively easy to cross by horse and cart at low tide. Not only that, but boats would sail upriver and downriver (at high tide) to moor near the gallows to get the best view possible. Such a laugh!

Eventually the dismal procession would arrive from either the Newgate or Marshalsea Prisons, led by the Admiral Marshal carrying a silver oar (to prove his authority). The pirate or pirates in question would be manacled in a heavily guarded cart, and they would sometimes chink their chains cheekily to the throng of leering Londoners who would hurl the most obscene abuse (and worse!) as they passed. It was a tradition for pirates to die with as much bravado as possible, so they would often dress in their finest clothes, festooned in red and blue ribbons. One even kicked his footwear into the crowd, joking that he could never be seen to die with his shoes on.

The gibbet at Execution Dock was a relatively simple affair—just two vertical posts and a cross member from which the rope or ropes would dangle. The pirate would be asked (not very nicely) to climb up a shortish ladder, where a noose would be put over his head. All the executioner had to do was pull the ladder away. Money for old rope! In those days hanging did not always kill the customer immediately, especially if their neck didn't break at the first drop, so it was quite common for relatives to swing on their nearest and dearest's legs to hasten his horrible end—a grisly sight, but just what the audience ordered. After the three tides had washed over them, the buccaneers' bodies would either be thrown into unmarked graves or hung up again in special cages. These were positioned along various parts of the river, until the bodies rotted to their bare bones—a warning to any other ordinary sailors who thought they might like a bit of light piracy.

The Kidd Gets It

In 1701 the body of the notorious villain Captain William Kidd, who'd been kept for a year in the hideous Newgate Prison, was hung on a special gibbet at Tilbury Point. He was put in a terrifying harness of iron hoops and chains, so that mariners could observe his rotting, crow-pecked corpse for more than an hour as they swept around that wide and desolate part of the Thames. Even more eerie, he'd been painted black all over, using the same tar with which they'd coat the bottoms of the ships, just so that he'd last longer. (Please don't try this on the dog.)

The cage was constructed of strong iron, firstly so that relatives couldn't steal the body to give it a decent burial and secondly so that the skeleton could be held in place once the flesh had rotted or been pecked away by the crows.

Across the Atlantic and around the Caribbean, it was a similar deal. Convicted pirates would dangle on special gibbets planted on the little outcrops. These poked above the water at the approaches to those Caribbean islands the pirates had terrorized for so long. On the East Coast, around Charleston, South Carolina, or Newport, Rhode Island, and particularly Boston, justice was short and swift, with pirates hung out like bunting at a fairground.

Sometimes, if the pirates knew that there was no escaping the rope, they went out fighting in great style. On one occasion in 1720, a pirate awaiting his death in the colony of Virginia demanded a bottle of wine and, as he swigged a glass, "Drank Damnation to the Governor and Confusion to the Colony."

In Britain between 1716 and 1726, over 400 convicted pirates were executed. The rest went to a fate that some thought even worse—they were imprisoned on dreaded hulks. These were decommissioned sloops and galleons that were moored in the vast lonely estuary of the Thames and used as prisons.

French Treat

Captured French corsairs (commissioned pirates) were often sent to these miserable Thames hulks where they were treated even worse. In 1797 one such prisoner was recorded as saying, "For the last eight weeks we have been reduced to eating dogs, cats, and rats . . . the only rations we get consist of moldy bread . . . rotten meat, and brackish water." That's rich, I reckon, coming from a country that gobbles up snails and the back legs off frogs at the drop of a chapeau, but we won't go into that now!

Forgotten

The Spanish pirate Antonio Mendoza had it even worse. The authorities of Saint Christopher in the West Indies cut off his ears, burned out his tongue with a red-hot iron, and left him literally to rot in a forgotten dungeon.

From around the middle of the eighteenth century, the general public didn't at all view pirates as heroes. Anyone who had to travel on the high seas would have been at their mercy. Pirates were generally regarded as enemies of all humankind, and it must be said that the relentless and savage hangings certainly acted as a deterrent to anyone contemplating answering a pirate help-wanted ad.

Timescale

Although the golden age for pirates was only really between the mid-seventeenth and the early eighteenth centuries, the very first hanging for robbery on the high seas was in 1228 and the very last as recently as 1840.

The End of the Voyage

The Golden Age of Piracy came to a speedy finale in the early nineteenth century when a massive $500,000 was set aside to create a special crack American squadron under Commodore David Porter. He put together eight superfast schooners, a newfangled steam-powered warship, and five flat-bottomed landing craft to attack the buccaneers when ashore. Last and most brilliant of all, he added the ultimate sitting duck—a ship that looked just like a ponderous old merchant vessel but that was packed with six massive cannons. With a gang of 1,500 tough marines, this little armada joined the six hard-worked U.S. warships that were already in the Caribbean searching for the bewildered buccaneers. In a couple of years, the game was up, hundreds of pirates were captured or killed, and the rest simply disappeared into thin air.

One of the very last acts of piracy in the Atlantic Ocean took place on September 20, 1832, when the pirate ship *Panda* intercepted an American brig, the *Mexican*. The U.S. ship just happened to be carrying $20,000 worth of silver bars to Argentina from the East Coast. When the pirates politely asked their captain, a mean-spirited fellow called Pedro Gilbert, what to do with the captives, he replied rather oddly, "dead cats don't mew, you know what to do"—obviously a feline version of the old pirate saying "dead men tell no tales." The pirate crew promptly relieved the ship of its silver, ordered the crew downstairs, chucked in a load of oil-soaked rags, battened down the hatches, and set fire to what they planned would become the poor innocents' floating coffin. The crew luckily broke out but cleverly kept the fire going until the pirate ship was over the horizon (just in case they came back). A few months later, Gilbert and company were caught loading slaves on the African coast by a British warship, which took them immediately to Boston and hanged 'em.

But that was then, and this is now. Piracy, I have to report, is back, and with a vengeance. Not as it was in the past—ragged brigands in romantic sailing ships, armed with cutlasses, muskets, and cannons and stuff—but highly professional criminals in high-speed cruisers, armed to the teeth with rocket launchers, careering around the Indian Ocean and the South China Sea, hijacking cargo boats and private yachts for all they're worth. There's not a parrot or a wooden leg in sight. Likewise, the prizes are also different—no Spanish gold or Aztec jewelry these days. According to international security agencies, modern pirates go after stuff they can move and sell easily: boring stuff like paint, rope, and household commodities. But the modern pirates are just as ruthless, often tying up the crew and leaving them on board their ship while it ploughs ahead through busy, congested waters. As a defense against this new surge in maritime crime, the International Maritime Bureau's Piracy Reporting Centre was set up in 1992 in Malaysia where owners and captains alike can telephone to report anything suspicious.

But it's kind of like trying to turn back the very sea they sail in. Wherever there is a defenseless vessel bobbing around on a big, lonely ocean, there will always be those who think it might be fun to teach them a lesson they'll never forget. I don't know about you, but I think that if we'd never had pirates, I, for one, would miss 'em.

PIRATE SPEAK

the Admiralty: the group of stuffy old officers who once had general authority over British naval affairs. This also refers to the courts and the system of laws that ruled the seas.

Barbary Coast: the northern coast of Africa, extending from Egypt to the Atlantic Ocean. The Barbary pirates wreaked havoc on Mediterranean shipping for 300 years.

buccaneer: a plundering, loot-taking person operating outside the law (no commission in sight!) in the West Indies

bully beef: the delicious (not!) pickled beef carried in barrels on board ship

Caribbean islands: various islands, such as Barbados, Jamaica, and Hispaniola, that lie in the Caribbean Sea and were among the main haunts of some of the world's worst pirates

commission: formal authorization to perform specific acts. In pirate speak, a commission gave the bearer the right to attack the ships belonging to the enemies of one's country.

corsair: a plundering, loot-taking person operating outside the law along the Barbary Coast

cutlass: a short, curved sword used by sailors and pirates

gibbet: an upright post with a projecting arm that was used to hang the bodies of executed criminals

heave-ho!: a phrase used by sailors and pirates pulling hard on a rope

Lord High Admiral: the top official in the British Admiralty (not a person to mess with!)

merchant ship: a privately owned vessel that carries cargo to sell or trade—the favorite prey of pirates, buccaneers, corsairs, and bad guys of all kinds

oakum: rope smothered in tar used to fill in gaps between a ship's planks (and horrid work it was)

parts of a ship: deck (the flat top); hold (the cargo area beneath the deck); hull (the curved bottom); mainmast (the tallest and most important spar, or pole)

press-gang: a group of oh-so-friendly men who are empowered to force other men into naval or pirate service

privateer: an armed private sailor licensed to attack enemy shipping. Broadly, privateers attacked pretty much anything they liked, more or less without fear of being chased by the law.

quartermaster: the officer in charge of the helm and navigation equipment (one of your more important ship colleagues)

Royal Navy: in Britain, the arm of the service devoted to maritime activities, including shipbuilding, operating naval stations, and training naval personnel. A lot of our favorite pirates started out in the Royal Navy, where they learned their trade but got very little pay.

schooner: a two-masted vessel, with a foremast and a mainmast that are placed nearly amidships

trade route: a sea-lane used by merchant ships. Usually, a trade route had known—though not always reliable—weather patterns

West Indies: a large group of Caribbean islands between North and South America

FURTHER READING

Black, Clinton V. *Pirates of the West Indies.* New York: Cambridge University Press, 1989.

Hague, Michael. *The Book of Pirates.* New York: HarperCollins Publishers, 2001.

Hawes, Charles Boardman. *The Dark Frigate.* New York: Little, Brown & Company, 1996.

Kallen, Stuart A. *Life Among the Pirates.* San Diego, CA: Lucent Books, 1999.

Lawrence, Iain. *The Buccaneers.* New York: Delacorte, 2001.

————. *The Smugglers.* New York: Delacorte, 1999.

————. *The Wreckers.* New York: Delacorte, 1998.

Lindgren, Astrid. *The Adventures of Pippi Longstocking.* New York: Viking Children's Books, 1997.

Meltzer, Milton. *Piracy and Plunder: A Murderous Business.* New York: Dutton Books, 2001.

Platt, Richard. *Eyewitness: Pirate.* New York: DK Publishing, 2000.

Sharp, Anne W. *Daring Women Pirates.* Minneapolis, MN: Lerner Publications Company, 2002.

Stevenson, Robert Louis. *Treasure Island.* New York: Atheneum, 1981.

Walker, Richard. *The Barefoot Book of Pirates.* Cambridge, MA: Barefoot Books, 1998.

Weatherly, Myra. *Women Pirates: Eight Stories of Adventure.* Greensboro, NC: Morgan Reynolds, 1998.

WEBSITES

General Information
Pyrate's Providence
   <http://www.inkyfingers.com/pyrates>
CyberInk Pirates!
   <http://www.yohoyoho.com>
The Pirate's Library
   <http://www.ferncanyonpress.com/pirates.html>
Pirates, Privateers, Swashbucklers, and Fops
   <http://www.legends.dm.net/index.html>

Pirates in Paradise
History of the Bahamas
   <http://www.geographia.com/bahamas>
Nassau Tourism
   <http://www.pirates-of-nassau.com>

Pirate Shipwrecks Discovered
Pirate Ghosts
   <http://www.discovery.com/stories/history/pirates/
   pirates.html>
Pirates of the Whydah
   <http://www.nationalgeographic.com/whydah/main.
   html>
Blackbeard's Queen Anne's Revenge
   <http://www.blackbeard.eastnet.ecu.edu/main.html>
Tales from the Deep
   <http://www.whyfiles.org/036pirates>
North Carolina Maritime Museum
   <http://www.ah.dcr.state.nc.us/qar>

INDEX

ABOUT THE AUTHOR

John Farman has worked as a commercial illustrator and a cartoonist and has written more than thirty nonfiction books for children. He lives in London, England.